OUT & ABOUT

• WALKING GUIDES TO BRITAIN •

No 4

Central England

MARSHALL CAVENDISH

First published in Great Britain in 1995 by
Marshall Cavendish Books, London
(a division of Marshall Cavendish Partworks Ltd)

Copyright © 1995 Marshall Cavendish

ISBN 03190 057 63

British Library Cataloguing in Publication Data:
A catalogue record for this book is available from the British Library

Printed and bound in Dubai, U.A.E.

Some of this material has previously appeared in the Marshall Cavendish partwork OUT & ABOUT

CONTENTS

Introduction to

OUT & ABOUT

• WALKING GUIDES TO BRITAIN •

Walking has become one of the most popular pastimes in Britain. To enjoy walking, you don't need any special skills, you don't have to follow rules or join expensive clubs, and you don't need any special equipment – though a pair of walking boots is a good idea! It is an easy way of relaxing and getting some exercise, and of enjoying nature and the changing seasons.

The OUT & ABOUT WALKING GUIDES TO BRITAIN will give you ideas for walks in your own neighbourhood and in other areas of Britain. All the walks are devised around a theme and range in length from about 2 to 9 miles (3.25 to 14.5 km) and in difficulty from very easy to mildly strenuous. Since each walk is circular, you will always be able to get back to your starting point.

Devised by experts and tested for accuracy, all the walks are accompanied by clear, practical instructions and an enlarged section of the relevant Ordnance Survey map. The flavour of the walk and highlights to look out for are described in the introductory text.

LOCAL COLOUR

Background features give you extra insight into items of local interest. The OUT & ABOUT WALKING GUIDES TO BRITAIN relate legends, point out unusual architectural details, provide a potted history of the lives of famous writers and artists connected with a particular place, explain traditional crafts still practised by local artisans, and uncover the secrets behind an ever-changing landscape.

DISCOVER NATURE

One of the greatest pleasures in going for a walk is the sense of being close to nature. On the walks suggested in the OUT & ABOUT WALKING GUIDES TO BRITAIN, you can feel the wind, smell the pine trees, hear the birds and see the beauty of the countryside. You will become more aware of the seasons – the life cycles of butterflies, the mating calls of birds, the protective behaviour of all creatures with their young. You will see the beginning of new life in the forests and fields, the bluebell carpets in spring woodlands, the dazzling beauty of rhododendron bushes in early summer, the swaying cornfields of summer and the golden colours of leaves in autumn. The OUT & ABOUT WALKING GUIDES TO BRITAIN tell you what to look out for and where to find it.

NATURE WALK

Occasional nature walk panels. will highlight an interesting feature that you will see on your walk. You will learn about natural and manmade details in the landscape, how to tell which animal or bird has nibbled the cones in a pine forest, what nurse trees are and what a triangulation point is.

FACT FILE

The fact file will give you at-a-glance information about each walk to help you make your selection.

✳	**general location**
OS	**map reference for Ordnance Survey**
	map with grid reference for starting point
	length of the walk in
	miles and kilometres
◕	**time needed if walking at an average speed**
▬	**character of the walk: easy/easy with**
◼	**strenuous parts/mildly strenuous; hills to**
▲	**be climbed and muddy or dangerous**
	areas are pointed out
P	**parking facilities near the start of the walk**
T	**public transport information**
🍺	**facilities for refreshment, including pubs**
🍴	**serving lunchtime meals, restaurants, tea**
	rooms and picnic areas
WC	**location of toilets**
⌐⌐	**historic sites**

miles 0 1 2 3 4 5 6 7 8 9
kms 0 1 2 3 4 5 6 7 8 9 10 11 12 13 14 15

ORDNANCE SURVEY MAPS

All the walks in the OUT & ABOUT WALKING GUIDES TO BRITAIN are illustrated on large-scale, full-colour maps supplied by the Ordnance Survey. Ordnance Survey are justifiably proud of their worldwide reputation for excellence and accuracy. For extra clarity, the maps have been enlarged to a scale of 1:21,120 (3 inches to 1 mile).

The route for each walk is marked clearly on the map with a broken red line, and the numbers along the

ABOVE: *Colourful narrowboats are always an attractive feature on inland waterways.*

route refer you to the numbered stages in the written directions. In addition, points of interest are marked on the maps with letters. Each one is mentioned in the walk directions and is described in detail in the introductory text.

COUNTRYWISE

The countryside is one of our greatest resources. If we treat it with respect, we can preserve it for the future.

Throughout the countryside there is a network of paths and byways. Some are former trading routes, others are simply the paths villagers took to visit one another in the days before public transport. Most are designated 'rights of way': foot-paths, open only to people on foot, and bridleways, open to people on foot, horseback or bicycle. These paths can be identified on Ordnance Survey maps and verified, in cases of dispute, by the definitive map for the area, held by the relevant local authority.

THE LAW OF TRESPASS

If you find a public right of way barred to you, you may remove the obstruction or take a short detour around it. However, in England and Wales, if you stray from the footpath you are trespassing and could be sued in a civil court for damages. In Scotland, rights of way are not recorded on definitive maps, nor is there a law of trespass. Although you may cross mountain and moorland paths, landowners are permitted to impose restrictions on access, such as during the grouse-shooting season, which should be obeyed.

If you are following a public right of way and find, for example, that your path is blocked by a field of crops, you are entitled to walk the line of the footpath through the crops, in single file. Farmers are required, by law, to restore public rights of way within 14 days of ploughing. However, if you feel uncomfortable about doing this and can find a way round, then do so. But report the matter to the local authority who will take the necessary action to clear the correct route.

RIGHT: *The stunning patchwork of fields surrounding the picturesque village of Widecombe in the heart of Dartmoor makes a beautiful setting for the famous annual fair.*
BELOW: *Brown hares boxing in spring are a fascinating sight.*

It is illegal for farmers to place a bull on its own in a field crossed by a right of way (unless the bull is not a recognized dairy breed). If you come across a bull alone in a field, find another way round.

COMMONS AND PARKS

There are certain areas in England and Wales where you may be able to wander without keeping to paths, such as most commons and beaches. There are also country parks, set up by local authorities for public recreation – parkland, woodland, heath or farmland.

The National Trust is the largest private landowner in England and Wales. Its purpose is to preserve areas of natural beauty and sites of historic interest by acquisition, holding them in trust for public access and enjoyment. Information on access may be obtained from National Trust headquarters at

THE COUNTRY CODE

- **Enjoy the countryside, and respect its life and work**

- **Always guard against risk of fire**

- **Fasten all gates**

- **Keep your dogs under close control**

- **Keep to public footpaths across farmland**

- **Use gates and stiles to cross fences, hedges and walls**

- **Leave livestock, crops and machinery alone**

- **Take your litter home**

- **Help to keep all water clean**

- **Protect wildlife, plants and trees**

- **Take special care on country roads**

- **Make no unnecessary noise**

36 QueenAnne's Gate, London SW1H 9AS
Tel: 071-222 9251.

Most regions of great scenic beauty in England and Wales are designated National Parks or Areas of Outstanding Natural Beauty (AONB). In Scotland, they are known as National Scenic Areas (NSAs) or AONBs.

Most of this land is privately owned and there is no right of public access. In some cases, local authorities may have negotiated agreements with landowners to allow walkers access on mountains and moors.

CONSERVATION
National park, AONB or NSA status is intended to provide some measure of protection for the land-scape, guarding against unsuitable development while encouraging enjoyment of its natural beauty.

ABOVE RIGHT *Carelessness with cigarettes, matches or camp fires can be devastating in a forest.*

Nature reserves are areas set aside for conservation. Most are privately owned, some by large organizations such as the Royal Society for the Protection of Birds. Although some offer public access, most require permission to enter.

THE RAMBLERS ASSOCIATION
The aims of the Ramblers Association are to further greater understanding and care of the countryside, to protect and enhance public rights of way and areas of natural beauty, to improve public access to the countryside, and to encourage more people to take up rambling as a healthy, recreational activity. It has played an important role in preserving and developing our national footpath network.

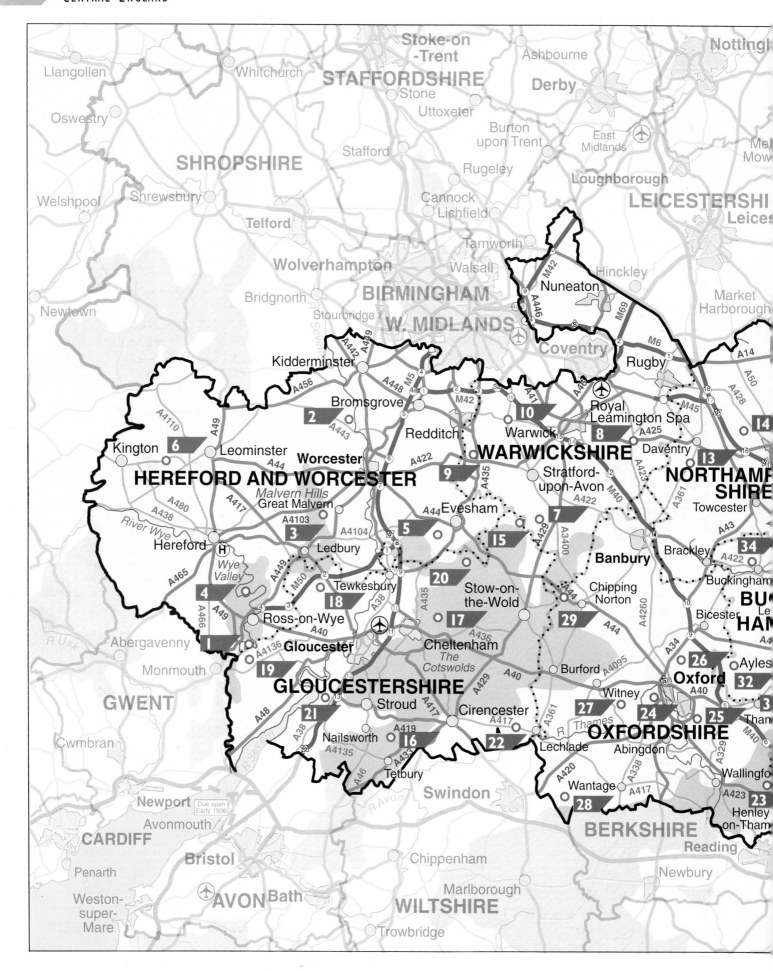

Central England

All the walks featured in this book are plotted and numbered on the regional map (left) and listed in the box below.

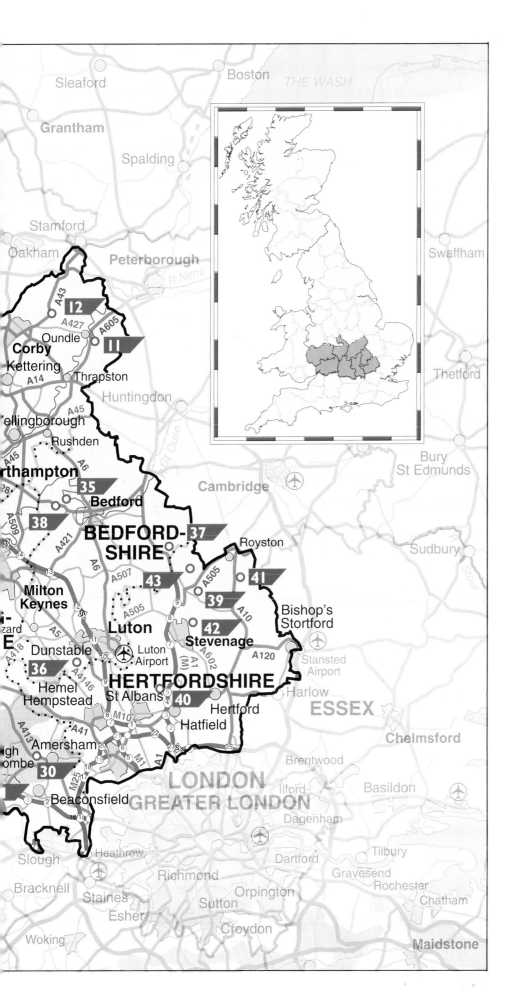

1 Coppet Hill & the Wye Valley
2 Round Shrawley Wood
3 On the Ridge Top
4 The Churches of the Wye
5 Bredon Hill
6 Black-and-White Lanes
7 Little Everest
8 Midland Waterways
9 Down Ryknild Street
10 Forest of Arden
11 Middle England River
12 Deene Park
13 Enclosures and Clearances
14 The Villages of Althorp
15 Cotswold Gardens
16 The Wool Trail
17 The Climb to Belas Knap
18 Redmarley
19 A Woodland Trail
20 Stanton and Snowshill
21 By Green, Manor and Court
22 Stone, Glass and Gravel
23 Beechwood Hills and Valleys
24 Happy Valley
25 A Hilltop Village
26 A Chequered Landscape
27 Stanton Harcourt
28 White Horse to White House
29 Rollright Rambles
30 Along Ancient Lanes
31 The Hellfire Walk
32 Overlooking the Vale
33 A Walk in Witchert Country
34 Fair, Majestic Paradise
35 To the Windmill
36 Butterfly Grasslands
37 Old Warden
38 A Tour of Turvey
39 Animal Farm
40 Parkland and Woodland
41 A Tale of Two Villages
42 A Walkern Walk
43 Seven Springs

USING MAPS

Although the OUT & ABOUT WALKING GUIDES TO BRITAIN give you all the information you need, it is useful to have some basic map skills. Most of us have some experience of using a motoring atlas to navigate by car. Navigating when walking is much the same, except that mistakes are much more time and energy consuming and, if circumstances conspire, could lead to an accident.

A large-scale map is the answer to identifying where you are. Britain is fortunate in having the best mapping agency in the world, the Ordnance Survey, which produces high-quality maps, the most popular being the 1:50,000 Landranger series. However, the most useful for walkers are the 1:25,000 Pathfinder, Explorer and Outdoor Leisure maps.

THE LIE OF THE LAND

A map provides more than just a bird's eye view of the land; it also conveys information about the terrain – whether marshy, forested, covered with tussocky grass or boulders; it distinguishes between footpaths and bridleways; and shows boundaries such as parish and county boundaries.

Symbols are used to identify a variety of landmarks such as churches, camp and caravan sites, bus, coach and rail stations, castles, caves and historic houses. Perhaps most importantly of all, the shape of the land is indicated by contour lines. Each line represents land at a specific height so it is possible to read the gradient from the spacing of the lines (the closer the spacing, the steeper the hill).

GRID REFERENCES

All Ordnance Survey maps are over-printed with a framework of squares known as the National Grid. This is a reference system which, by breaking the country down into squares, allows you to pinpoint any place in the country and give it a unique reference number; very useful when making rendezvous arrangements. On OS Landranger, Pathfinder and Outdoor Leisure maps it is possible to give a reference to an accuarcy of 100 metres. Grid squares on these maps cover an area of 1 km x 1 km on the ground.

GIVING A GRID REFERENCE

Blenheim Palace in Oxfordshire has a grid reference of **SP 441 161.** This is constructed as follows:

SP These letters identify the 100 km grid square in which Blenheim Palace lies. These squares form the basis of the National Grid. Information on the

100 km square covering a particular map is always given in the map key.

441 161 This six figure reference locates the position of Blenheim Palace to 100 metres in the 100 km grid square.

44 This part of the reference is the number of the grid line which forms the western (left-hand) boundary of the 1 km grid square in which Blenheim Palace appears. This number is printed in the top and bottom margins of the relevant OS map (Pathfinder 1092 in this case).

16 This part of the reference is the number of the grid line which forms the southern (lower) boundary of the 1 km grid square in which Blenheim Palace appears. This number is printed in the left- and right-hand margins of the relevant OS map (Pathfinder 1092).

These two numbers together (SP 4416) locate the bottom left-hand corner of

the 1 km grid square in which Blenheim Palace appears. The remaining figures in the reference **441 161** pinpoint the position within that square by dividing its western boundary lines into tenths and estimating on which imaginary tenths line Blenheim Palace lies.

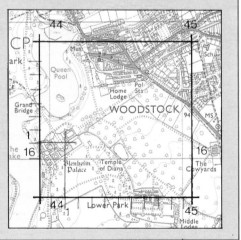

COPPET HILL & THE WYE VALLEY

From castle ruins to a magnificent river gorge

In a southern corner of unspoilt Herefordshire, the beautiful River Wye meanders gracefully through the countryside, forming the border between Herefordshire and Gloucestershire. This is the start of the famous scenic gorge where the river flows swiftly below craggy cliffs and steep wooded slopes, making large horseshoe meanders on its way from the busy market town of Ross-on-Wye, past historic Monmouth, to join the River Severn beyond Chepstow.

Coppet Hill is a familiar and distinctive landmark of extensive size in this part of the Wye valley and from its summit at 617 feet (188 metres) there are panoramic views

PAUL FELIX. INSET: STEPHEN DALTON/NHPA

FACT FILE

* Coppet Hill, Wye valley, South Herefordshire

* Pathfinder 1087 (SO 41/51), grid reference SO 576197

miles 0 1 2 3 4 5 6 7 8 9 10 miles
kms 0 1 2 3 4 5 6 7 8 9 10 11 12 13 14 15 kms

* Allow 3½ hours

* Easy route with one climb, but not suitable for children. Do not attempt the walk when the River Wye is in flood, as the second half of the walk is along the river bank. Check at the Countryside Service hut at the car park before starting out. Wear walking boots or strong shoes

* **P** Goodrich Castle. Picnic site clearly signed from all approach roads

* **WC** Toilets and refreshments at car park, and inn at Goodrich

* Goodrich Castle. Open daily from April to September. Closed on Mondays the rest of the year. Admission charge

across the wonderful Wye valley, designated as an Area of Outstanding Natural Beauty.

Until quite recently no public access was allowed across the hill, but since the formation of the Coppet Hill Common Trust, delightful paths have been maintained and waymarked by wardens of the Wye Valley Countryside Service.

THE IMPRESSIVE CASTLE

The walk starts from an attractive picnic site next to the well-preserved Goodrich Castle. From here a short stretch of minor road offers splendid glimpses of the Wye, before reaching a waymarked path leading up and over Coppet Hill. Within 2 miles (3.2 km) the undulating route

▲ *A spectacular view of Coppet Hill and the Wye from Symond's Yat. (inset) Fruit is the staple diet of the yellow-necked mouse. (below) Goodrich Castle.*

PAUL FELIX

GOODRICH - COPPET HILL

This walk starts from the picnic site next to Goodrich Castle **Ⓐ**.

1 From the picnic site follow a tarmac lane leading to Goodrich village. Here turn left along a road to Welsh Bicknor until it forms an unusual 'Dry Arch', bridging another road below. Continue ahead looking left for views of Kerne Bridge **Ⓑ** and gradually ascending until reaching the first turn on the right at the foot of Coppet Hill.

2 Behind the grass island at the road turning stands a Coppet Hill Common notice board indicating the start of three waymarked paths across the hill. The walk follows a green-arrowed route which climbs a series of wooden steps, twisting and turning through woodland and past huge stone boulders. At a junction it bears left, then right, before leading on to the open hillside, where a triangulation point **Ⓒ** marks the height of 617 feet (188 metres). From here, continue uphill to reach the remains of a stone folly **Ⓓ**.

3 Keep the remains of the folly on the left, and follow the wide level path near a wood and with glimpses of a boundary wall. Soon a gentle descent of 1½ miles (2.4 km) begins, first along an open ridge then more steeply through woodland. Cross a stile and continue across a field to the bank of the River Wye, opposite Coldwell Rocks **Ⓔ**.

4 At the riverside turn right, following a definitive path through meadows and

along the bank of the Wye until a field gate leads on to a track through trees. Pass through another gate where a sign directs a way to 'Coppet Hill Only'. Here leave the waymarked route by bearing left to re-join the riverside path leading to Huntsham bridge **Ⓕ**.

5 At Huntsham bridge turn right on to the road and follow it to a T-junction. Here, bear right along a busier road to Goodrich, and after 450 yards (405 metres), opposite a hedged track, turn left through a kissing gate (the footpath sign is missing). Now follow an undefined route which goes diagonally right across a field to a stile marked with a yellow arrow. Cross this and continue in the same direction through the next field to a gateway leading on to a short track which leads to the roadside at Goodrich.

6 Turn right along this road and beyond the Old Vicarage turn left up some narrow steps. At the top, a gate signed 'to the church' leads on to a wide, grass-covered path taking you into the churchyard of St Giles' Church **Ⓖ**. Keep right of the church along a well-used route, which goes through a kissing gate, across a field to another kissing gate. In the next field bear diagonally right and descend to a further gate leading into Goodrich School playing field. Walk straight across this to a final gate leading on to the road. Turn left past the school, cross the road ahead and retrace your way back up the lane to Goodrich Castle picnic site at the end of the walk.

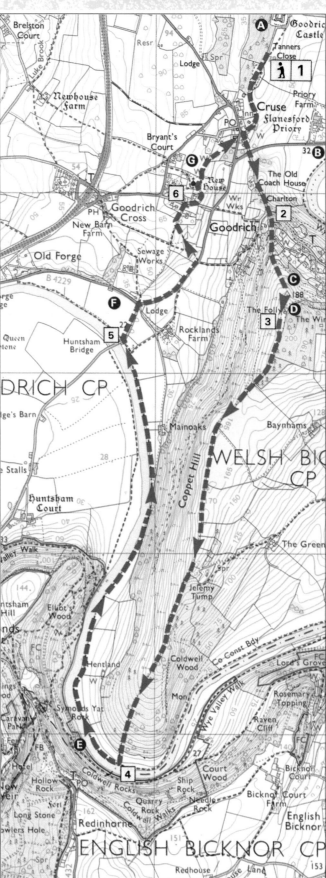

THE WALK

descends to the banks of the river, shadowed here by the lofty heights of Symond's Yat Rock and the Coldwell Rocks on the opposite bank.

The walk continues along a definitive right of way, following a delightful stretch of the River Wye for a further 1½ miles (1.6 km) till meeting Huntsham bridge. The remainder of the walk continues on pleasant paths and quiet lanes through Goodrich village with its historic church of St Giles.

◄ *The ruined folly on Coppet Hill is covered with brambles and ferns. It is a perfect spot for adders. (above) Kerne Bridge spans the winding River Wye.*

One of the main attractions of this walk is the impressive ruin of Goodrich Castle **Ⓐ**, founded in the 11th century by the Normans to defend the Welsh borders. The Marcher Lords, as they were known, selected a superb site guarding an ancient river crossing. However, unlike other border castles, its strength was never tested and having served its purpose, it became unoccupied at the beginning of the 17th century. It was reused for a short time during the Civil War, but in 1646 it fell into ruins, and, eventually, in 1920, it was placed in the care of the State.

THE WYE VALLEY

After leaving the castle, the route proceeds to the village of Goodrich. There is a scenic view between trees to the left of Kerne Bridge **Ⓑ** spanning the River Wye far below. This fine stone bridge was constructed in 1828 after the passing of an Act of Parliament 'for building a bridge over the Wye'.

From the top of the steps a well trodden path leads between shoulder high bracken, bushes of golden gorse, waving willow herb and young saplings of oak, hazel and birch. At the triangulation point **Ⓒ** there are splendid views of the Wye valley. The River Wye shimmers as it flows around Goodrich and under Huntsham and Kerne bridges. Ahead, pretty white-washed cottages dot the hilly slopes of the Great Doward above Symond's Yat, and on a clear day the Welsh hills can be seen in the far distance.

At the summit of Coppet Hill stand the overgrown remains of a folly **Ⓓ**, built long ago as a summer house where in the 18th century gentlemen enjoyed the outstanding scenery below.

Depending on the time of year, a

Coldwell Rocks rise dramatically above the River Wye and provide nesting sites for rare peregrine falcons.

variety of wild flowers grow beside the path, including primroses, violets, orchids, harebells and willow herb. Carpets of bluebells can be seen in the coppiced woodland.

The steep descent from Coppet Hill leads to a wonderful site where the River Wye flows below the lofty heights of Coldwell Rocks **Ⓔ**. In spring and early summer, rare

Joshua Cristall

Joshua Cristall was a notable water-colour artist who is associated with Goodrich and Coppet Hill. His early 19th-century paintings clearly depict his love of the countryside, especially the Wye valley.

Born in Cornwall in 1767, Joshua Cristall first started painting there. He then worked as a design painter for a china manufacturer in Shropshire before training at the Royal Academy Schools.

He first visited the Wye valley in 1802 while on a sketching tour, but it was another 20 years before Cristall and his wife settled in Goodrich. Here he remained until the death of his wife, when he returned to London, leaving instructions that when he died he wished to be buried beside her at Goodrich.

Although unsuccessful in selling his work, he was considered a talented enough artist to become a founder member of the Old Water Colour Society, serving as President three times, and also becoming President of the Royal Institute of Painters in Water Colours. He was a highly gifted artist who produced sketches, oils and watercolours of classical and

HEREFORD CITY MUSEUM

A charming rural scene on Coppet Hill sketched by the artist, Joshua Cristall.

rural scenes, including fine views of Coppet Hill, Goodrich, Coldwell Rocks and Ross. An exhibition of his work was shown in the Victoria and Albert Museum in 1975, and a collection of his paintings are housed at Hereford City Art Gallery. Cristall died in 1847 and his grave may be seen on the north side of St Giles' church in Goodrich.

peregrine falcons steal the scene with their dramatic flying displays as they smoothly glide and dive from their inaccessible nesting sites.

Along this delightful stretch of river there is much to see. Graceful swans, busy ducks and energetic canoeists paddle through the silent gorge, while high above, at Symond's Yat Rock, crowds of visitors eagerly admire the Wye's famous horseshoe bend below.

Walking below the bracken-clad slopes of Coppet Hill, the bridge at Huntsham **F** and Goodrich church spire come into view.

THE VILLAGE CHURCH

The unique metal road bridge was built in 1885 by the neighbouring Courtfield Estate. It replaced an ancient ferry known in the 18th century as Hanson Rope.

Roads and field paths now lead to Goodrich, a picturesque village. The church dedicated to St Giles **G** has a tall spire which provides a distinctive landmark throughout this walk. Although the church is usually locked, a key is available from an address shown in the porch. The water-colour artist, Joshua Cristall, is buried here. After visiting the church, take the path past an ivy-covered well to return to Goodrich Castle.

BOTH PHOTOS: PAUL FELIX

▲ *The 19th-century metal road bridge at Huntsham. (right) St Giles Church with its handsome broach spire stands in an elevated position near fields.*

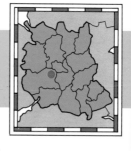

ROUND SHRAWLEY WOOD

Alongside the River Severn and around an ancient wood

This short walk combines farm-land, river bank, woodland and parkland. It is a near-perfect miniature, with unspectacular but diverse features. The walk begins and ends at Shrawley church, which mostly dates from the 12th century.

From the church you descend to the Severn, Britain's longest river, passing Court Farm which was the old manor house. Just below the farm are several artificial mounds known jointly as 'Oliver's Mound', which seem to be part of an old for-tification defending a river crossing.

RIVER TRAFFIC

Soon afterwards you pass an out-crop of New Red Sandstone **Ⓐ** — the stone of which the church is con-structed. A swampy area next to the river **Ⓑ** contains plants such as bal-sam. Walking along the river, you will see a variety of passing traffic, from swans to barges.

Leaving the Severn behind, the path takes you a short way up the valley of the Dick Brook. It is now almost impossible to believe that 300 years ago this was an important industrial site. The lower Severn Valley, from the Forest of Dean in the south to the side valley of the Stour, leading up to the Birmingham area, was the heart of England's iron industry. Forges used charcoal from

DAVID HUNTER. INSET: NIGEL DENNIS/NHPA

FACT FILE

- ✳ Shrawley, Worcestershire, 5 ½ miles (9 km) west of Droitwich

- ▣ Pathfinder 974 (SO 86/96) with a short stretch on 973 (SO 66/76), grid reference SO 806647

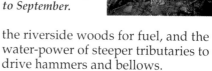

miles 0   1   2   3   4   5   6   7   8   9   10 miles
kms 0 1 2 3 4 5 6 7 8 9 10 11 12 13 14 15 kms

- ◔ Allow 2–3 hours

- ▬ Mostly easy walking. Some woodland sections may be muddy after rain, so walking boots are recommended

- 🅿 Roadside parking on minor road at entrance to Shrawley church

- 🍴 New Inn (food, garden) in Shrawley

DAVID HUNTER

◀ *Court Farm, seen from the farm track shortly before you reach the Severn, was originally the old manor house.*

▲ *The River Severn skirts the woods at Shrawley. The Monkey flower (inset) thrives in wet places and flowers from July to September.*

the riverside woods for fuel, and the water-power of steeper tributaries to drive hammers and bellows.

STREAM POWER

Where the Dick Brook joined the river **Ⓒ** there was a lock and exten-sive wharves, at which cargo was transferred to small boats which could go up the Brook. There used to be another lock halfway between here and the stepping-stones where you cross the stream **Ⓓ**. These were at the site of a forge, with another wharf, and power was provided by a millpond further upstream.

From the Dick Brook, the path follows a shaded side valley up into Shrawley Wood, which the route skirts round. This luxuriant wood of

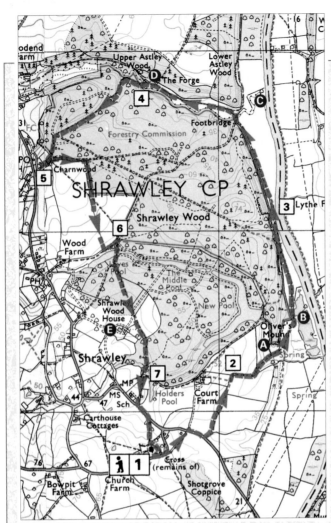

SHRAWLEY AND THE RIVER SEVERN

The walk begins at the entrance to Shrawley churchyard.

▶ With the church behind you, turn left along the road to a bend. Turn right through the left of two gates and walk down the side of the field to reach the main road by the stile. Turn right on the road for 100 yards (90 metres), then left over the stile. Keep close to the hedge on the left for 40 yards (36 metres), then turn left through the gate into the second field. Follow the hedge on the left and at the far left corner go over the stile.

▶ Turn right on the track, then go through the gate and continue across the field on the clear vehicle track. This crosses a minor stream, and becomes a footpath, passing the New Red Sandstone outcrop **A**. The path veers left and across a field to a gap (between a fence on the left and trees on the right), leading to a meadow **B** alongside the River Severn. Follow the river bank to reach a gate leading to a short section of track.

▶ Go through a second gate into another riverside meadow. The footpath keeps close to the wood on the left, and eventually curves away from the river just before the point at which it is joined by the Dick Brook **C**. At the far left corner, go over the stile and then immediately right to cross the brook by a footbridge. Go on for 40 yards (36 metres), then left on a track up the valley for ⅓ mile (500 metres). At the end of the field on the left, turn left on the footpath and walk down the side of the field to a stile.

▶ Go down the steps, recross Dick Brook by the very solid stepping-stones **D** and bear right. The path ascends the side of the valley, and then turns left into a side valley; ignore the faint path that continues up Dick Brook. Follow the side valley uphill to the crest of the ridge, then go left and uphill. Go over the rise and then descend to a vehicle track. Turn right through a gate and follow the access road to reach the New Inn and the post office at the road junction.

▶ Return up the access road and into the wood. Keep straight on, following the wide vehicle track to the right of the way you came, until the field on the right ends; then turn right through the gap in the fence and go down the left-hand side of the field. When the wood on the left ends, go through the gap in the fence ahead and continue on the vehicle track between two fields.

About 20 yards (18 metres) short of Layes Pool at the bottom of the valley, turn left along a vehicle track around the lake, leading to a gate into the wood.

▶ Turn sharp right 30 yards (27 metres) after the gate, onto another track, which crosses the dam at the end of the lake and continues through a wood to a fieldgate and stile, ahead. Here you enter the park around Shrawley Wood House and bear left, uphill, away from the obvious track, which goes ahead from the gate. As soon as the house comes into view **E**, aim left of it for a stile in the fence ahead. Cross the avenue of trees to the next stile at the corner of the paddock, and then to the gate just to the left of the far right corner of the paddock. Continue across the latter to a gate into the wood, near the far right-hand corner. Enter the wood, going forward and downhill to the footbridge.

▶ Cross the stream and go over the stile into a field. Cross the field by a sunken path to another stile, then continue on a path between hedges to reach the road. Turn left and continue for 100 yards (90 metres), and then turn right through a kissing gate. Go uphill, following an avenue of lime trees to a gate into the churchyard, then left and uphill. Curve round the church to the porch and out to the road.

DAVID HUNTER

about 500 acres (200 hectares) is notable for the small-leaved lime trees, native to Britain, which form the underwood. It abounds with ramson (wild garlic) and also contains the rare wood fescue grass.

The final section of the walk goes through the grounds of the 19th-century Shrawley Wood House **E**, passing an artificial lake and crossing a fine avenue of beeches.

▶ *This tranquil area was the site of a forge for the iron industry 300 years ago.*

ON THE RIDGE TOP

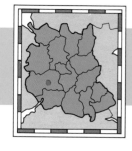

◄ *From the Lady Howard de Walden Drive, on the hills above Malvern, there are fine views towards Hereford and Wales to the west. This area is a haunt of the great spotted woodpecker (inset).*

From a spa town to a magnificent viewpoint on the Malvern Hills

Little Malvern, Malvern Wells, Great Malvern, Malvern Link, North Malvern and West Malvern are the six settlements that have grown up around the foot of the great ridge of the Malvern Hills. This walk is from Great Malvern, but looks down over Malvern Link, North Malvern and West Malvern. The hills, rising steeply from the Worcestershire and Herefordshire Plain, are some of the most distinctive landmarks of the Midlands and consist of hard rock, 600 million years old — the oldest in England.

LINKS WITH THE ARTS

The Priory Park and its fine Winter Gardens **A** nestle in the shadow of the hills. In the Park is a bronze bust of Sir Edward Elgar, who lived in Malvern and composed many of his finest works here, including the *Enigma Variations* and *The Dream of Gerontius*. Music and theatre have had long links with the town, and a regular supporter of the theatre was George Bernard Shaw, who wrote his play *The Apple Cart* for the first Malvern Festival in 1929.

The granite of the Malvern Hills was quarried in many places, leaving unsightly disused quarries **B**, but all work has now been stopped to preserve the hillside. The Malvern Hills Conservators, one of the first organized conservation groups in the world, have been looking after these hills since 1884.

The summit of the Worcestershire Beacon **C** at 1,396 feet (425 metres) is the highest land in this area and on a clear day the surrounding views are spectacular. Looking to the east, the Cotswold scarp, Bredon Hill and the towers and spires of churches are prominent. To the west is Wales and southwards is the outline of the old British Camp, an Iron Age fort on the top of the Herefordshire Beacon.

TAKING THE WATERS

Malvern has also achieved fame for its spring water, which is on sale throughout the world. The crystal-clear water can be sampled on this walk directly from a spring **D**. During the Victorian era, Malvern became popular as a spa town. Donkeys were available to carry the visitors up to the Beacon. Some of the old donkey stables **E** survive at the top of St Ann's Road. Other Victorian relics can be seen on Great Malvern station, which was built as a showpiece in the 1860s.

JOHN HESELTINE. INSET: PETER WILSON/NATURAL IMAGE

FACT FILE

- ☀ Great Malvern, 8 miles (12.8 km) south-west of Worcester and 10 miles (16 km) from M50 and M5

- 🗺 Pathfinder 1018 (SO 64/74), grid reference SO 778457

  | miles 0 | 1 | 2 | 3 | 4 | 5 | 6 | 7 | 8 | 9 | 10 miles |
  | kms 0 | 1 2 3 4 5 6 7 8 9 10 11 12 13 14 15 kms |

- 🕐 2½ hours

- ▬ Well-made paths that are dry and easy for walking. Steep ascent up side of the Malvern ridge, not suitable for children

- 🅿 Several car parks in Great Malvern. Excellent starting point is the Southlea coach and car park just uphill from the station, adjacent to the swimming pool and Priory Park

- 🚉 Great Malvern

- 🍴 Cafés in Great Malvern and snack bar at St Ann's Well

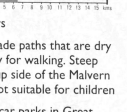

THE WALK

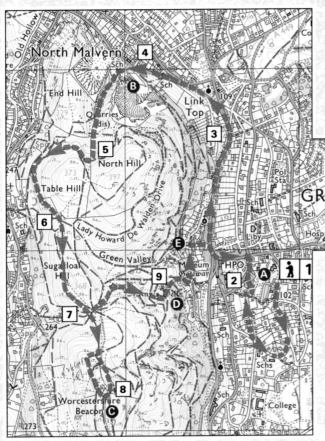

GREAT MALVERN

The walk begins at Southlea car park on Priory Road.

1 Facing the swimming pool building, turn left out of the car park and continue along Priory Road. Follow the bend round to the right, with glimpses of the famous boys' school (Malvern College) on the left, until you reach Orchard Road. On the corner is a rare Victorian pillar box dating from 1857, fluted in the shape of a Greek pillar. Walk along Orchard Road, into Priory Park and to the Winter Gardens **A**, where there is a café and toilets, as well as a cinema and theatre. Through the Winter Gardens is the Tourist Information Centre.

2 Turn right out of the Winter Gardens, then left uphill past the shops on Church Street, the main street of Malvern. At the top of this street bear right (signpost to Bromyard) and follow the road for a few hundred paces.

3 Fork left along the West Malvern and Bromyard Road, with a thatched house on the left and public toilets on the right. Opposite Holy Trinity Church are the old town stocks and whipping post, surrounded by an iron fence; behind them, in the trees, is the animal pound used for holding stray sheep from the Malvern Hills.

4 Further along this road, just past the Clock Tower, there is a signpost pointing to North Hill, Table and Sugar Loaf Hills. Go up the steps between the two old quarries **B**. After the first steps the way divides —

the left-hand route has wider views, but both routes rejoin higher up. The quarry to your left has been planted and partially concealed by trees, while there is vegetation growing on the steep rocks of the quarry on the right. The stony path leads up above the trees out onto the open hillside. Worcester Cathedral can be clearly seen on the flat plain to the north-east of the hills. Continue on up the steep slope. Near two hawthorn trees you will reach a broad, horizontal track wide enough for a car. This is the Lady Howard de Walden Drive and you can sit on a bench here and admire the views — from north-west to north-east, past Abberley Hill and the Clee Hills.

5 Turn right and follow this driveway round the hill; the view to the west will come into sight, revealing that Herefordshire is not as flat as the Worcestershire Plain. Small hills and valleys, looking lush and green, stretch out towards the Welsh hills. Where the drive splits, the right fork descends towards West Malvern, but you fork left, diagonally up the hill and can soon look down on the rooftops of West Malvern.

6 The track bends round to the left and at the gap or col, where the Worcestershire side of the hill comes into sight again, turn right to walk over the

small hill called Sugar Loaf. Follow the ridge top, unless it is too windy — which is quite likely. There are three paths, so you can go along the exposed top, or take the path on the sheltered side of the ridge.

7 Straight ahead is the summit of the Worcestershire Beacon, but first you drop down to the hollow where numerous paths meet at a large stone route indicator built out of the local rock. Take the broad path (grassy at first and then becoming stony) up round to the right of the Beacon **C**, which leads to the triangulation pillar, the toposcope or viewpoint.

8 Walk northwards, back to the large indicator stone, then follow the sign to St Ann's Well. Descend to a large stony track which follows the side of a delightful tree-filled valley, called Happy Valley.

9 Where the broad path splits, left into Happy Valley and right to St Ann's Well, go straight ahead for a few paces to admire the view, before going right to St Ann's Well. Here there is a café and a spring **D** from which you can taste the pure Malvern water. Beyond the café the zigzag path leads down to a narrow road. Turn left along this and at the T-junction look up to the left and you will see the wooden sheds which were the donkey stables **E**. Then turn right and go down the hill into the centre of Great Malvern. Retrace your steps down Church Street, perhaps paying a visit to the Priory Church on the way back to the car park to conclude the walk.

THE CHURCHES OF THE WYE

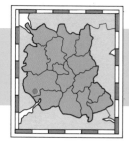

PAUL FELIX

A Wye Valley ramble linking four interesting churches

▲*Caple Thump, covered here with spring daffodils, was once the site of a Norman motte and bailey. Behind, is the Church of St John the Baptist. Wall pellitory (below right) grows nearby.*

Between the cathedral city of Hereford and the market town of Ross-on-Wye, the River Wye loops through undulating farmland. This circular walk explores the valley's delightful countryside and visits four contrasting churches on both sides of the river.

CAPLE THUMP

The Church of St John the Baptist **Ⓐ** in King's Caple is set on a hill above a bend in the Wye Valley. Its 14th-century tower and slender spire make it a familiar landmark, and there is a wonderful view from the churchyard. Opposite the church is Caple Thump, a wooded mound that was once the site of a Norman motte and bailey. Later, it was used as a site for village fairs and

festivities, a tradition recently revived by the local school.

A gentle descent from the church along a quiet lane leads to the Wye, and a crossing over Hoarwithy road-bridge **Ⓑ**. Here, there is a charming scene of gliding swans, noisy ducks and, occasionally, a darting, flashing kingfisher among the reeds and willows. Fishermen try their luck at catching the Wye's famous salmon, and canoeists paddle their way swiftly downstream or battle against the current.

HORSE FERRY

There has been a river-crossing here since at least the 14th century, when 'Hoarwithy Passage' had a ferry known as the 'Horse Ferry', which transported passengers, goods and livestock. In 1856, a timber toll-bridge was built. This was replaced 20 years later by an iron structure, which lasted until 1990, when the present bridge was built. No toll has been payable since 1935, but the tall toll-house still remains.

Hoarwithy itself is a pretty village, with attractive houses and cottages dotted along steep, wooded banks. Although the village lies within the parish of Hentland, the building of the bridge created a larger settlement, and a splendid new church, St Catherine's **Ⓒ**, was built

FACT FILE

⚹ King's Caple, 4 miles (6.4km) north-west of Ross-on-Wye

▭ Pathfinder 1064 (SO 42/52), grid reference SO 558288

miles 0 1 2 3 4 5 6 7 8 9 10 miles
kms 0 1 2 3 4 5 6 7 8 9 10 11 12 13 14 15 kms

◔ Allow up to 5 hours

▬ Undulating terrain; one steep ascent and descent. Suitable for all ages

🅿 Outside King's Caple's church

🍴 New Harp Inn, Hoarwithy; Lough Pool Inn, Sellack. Light refreshments at Pengethley Garden Centre

A CLEAVER/NATURE PHOTOGRAPHERS

THE WALK

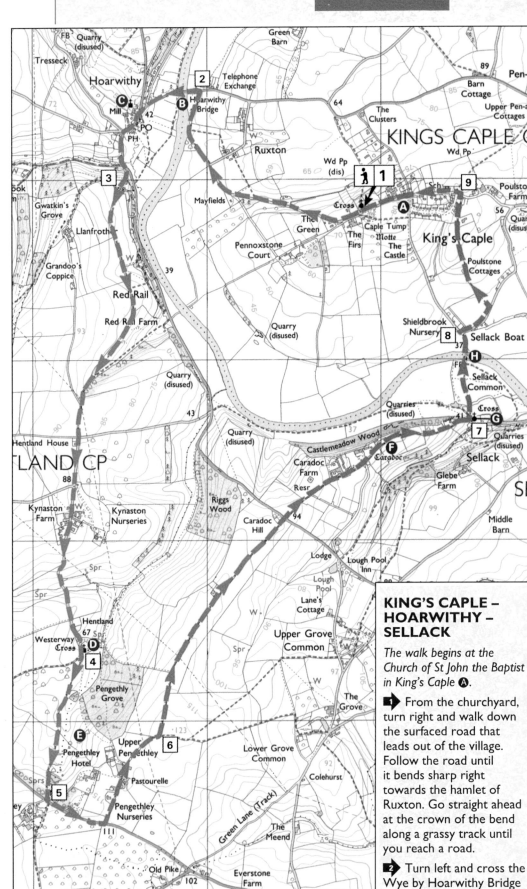

B. Continue into the village. Opposite a phone box, take a flight of steps leading up to Hoarwithy's church **C**. Return down the steps, and follow the road signposted to Ross-on-Wye. Cross over a stream. Just beyond a stone house called The Salmons, turn right on a signed footpath up a steep, wooded slope to a house called Quarry Bank.

3 Continue ahead across a farm track and over a rickety gate. Follow a hedge on your right through a long field. Cross a stile in the corner. At the end of another field, you reach a stile and gate leading to a sunken lane. Under the power line, this joins a farm track; bear left. Where a surfaced lane crosses by the old school, which is now Hentland House, go straight ahead along a surfaced lane to Hentland's church **D**.

4 Go through a kissing-gate to the right of the church into Pengethley Park **E**. Follow the path straight ahead past a pond on your left and over a waymarked stile. Walk ahead along a line of trees marking a former field boundary, then past another pond on your left until you reach a road.

5 Turn left on this busy road, passing the entrances to Pengethley Hotel and Garden Centre, then go sharp left along an unsigned bridleway used as a farm drive. Surfaced at first, this becomes an unmade track after passing the farm entrance and a small duck pond. Continue ahead past a derelict shack.

6 Where you reach open fields, the track bears right,

KING'S CAPLE – HOARWITHY – SELLACK

*The walk begins at the Church of St John the Baptist in King's Caple **A**.*

1 From the churchyard, turn right and walk down the surfaced road that leads out of the village. Follow the road until it bends sharp right towards the hamlet of Ruxton. Go straight ahead at the crown of the bend along a grassy track until you reach a road.

2 Turn left and cross the Wye by Hoarwithy Bridge

◄*St Catherine's, Hoarwithy, is an interesting 19th-century church built in the medieval Italian style. The River Wye (right) sweeps majestically between verdant banks that make a fine picnic spot.*

in the village in the 1880s.

The only church of its kind in this part of the world, a flight of stone steps ascends below overhanging evergreens to a campanile tower. A cloister walk leads to the entrance porch of an exceptional Italianate interior, which combines marble columns and mosaic floors with traditional English, carved-wood choir stalls, and stained-glass windows.

The man responsible for this remarkable building was the Reverend William Poole, vicar of Hentland and Hoarwithy from 1854 to 1901. He commissioned a London architect, J P Seddon, to design it around a formerly plain chapel. Poole's influence can be seen in other buildings nearby, including the reading room beside the church.

FINE VIEWPOINT

The walk follows field paths, climbing above the village to a viewpoint over the Wye Valley, from which the churches of King's Caple, Hoarwithy and Sellack are visible.

◄*Hentland's church incorporates work from the 13th and 14th centuries in its fabric. The once impressive, 17th-century mansion at Caradoc (below right) was gutted by fire in 1986.*

The nearby farmhouse of Llanfrother was reputedly the site of a 6th-century monastic college founded by St Dubricius. As you pick up a surfaced road at Kynaston, you pass Poole's school and vicarage, both now converted into houses. At the end of the lane is Hentland church **D**, dedicated to St Dubricius.

Surrounded by weathered tombs and ancient, gnarled yews, this remote building is thought to be the earliest foundation in the area. There are some traces of 13th-century work, a square 14th-century tower and some fading, 17th-century wall-paintings. The interior was much restored by Seddon in the 1850s. If the church is locked, the key may be obtained from Westway, a nearby cottage. Carpets of snowdrops make the churchyard most

but you turn left along a well-defined bridleway. About 1 mile (1.6km) along this, you cross the Hoarwithy road at Caradoc Hill. (A right turn here leads to the Lough Pool Inn ¼ mile (400m) away.) Continue on the bridleway, past racing stables and the charred remains of Caradoc Court **F**, then descending to Sellack's church **G**, with the track rough in places.

7 To the left of the church, an unsigned, but well-trodden path over the common leads to Sellack suspension footbridge **H**, where you cross the Wye.

8 At Sellack Boat, turn right past a couple of cottages on the right, then follow a signed footpath to the left across a field to a hedge. Continue with the hedge on your left to the top of a field. Follow a waymark over a stile to your left, and continue with a fence on your right. At the end of the fence, bear diagonally right to a metal gate and stile. A stony track leads to a road.

9 Turn left through King's Caple to return to your starting point.

Cakes and Ale

The parishes of Hentland, King's Caple and Sellack, with their four churches, all share a curious Palm Sunday tradition that dates back to 1484. In that year, one Thomas More, a wealthy vicar of the parish of Sellack, died having willed that:

'Bread and Ale to the value of 6s

Pax Cakes are given out, with cider or tea, to the parishoners of Hentland, King's Caple and Sellack on Palm Sunday.

and 8d be distributed to all and singular in the aforesaid churches for the good of my soul'.

Over the centuries, the founder's name was forgotten so that, by Victorian times, the charity, although given as a peace gift, was recorded as having been left by an unknown donor. It was distributed on Palm Sunday in the form of plain bread cakes, which were known as Pax Cakes. These were served with ale and accompanied by the greeting, 'Peace and good neighbourhood'. Taking part in this ceremony was seen as 'evidence of a desire to lay aside all enmities in order to prepare for the Easter Festival'.

The tradition still survives. Today, Pax Cakes are distributed with cider, tea or other refreshments. More's bequest, which was munificent in its day, is now worth only 33 pence a year. This goes towards the cost of producing the cakes, and all the parishioners of the three parishes are invited to participate in this special Palm Sunday tradition.

an idyllic setting near the banks of the Wye. In the churchyard, gravestones cluster around a graceful churchyard cross. These used to be standard features in English medieval churches, but the great majority were destroyed in the Civil War and its aftermath.

RESTORED CHURCH

The recently restored spire on the 14th-century tower is topped with a golden weathercock. Inside the unusually shaped building is a Jacobean gallery and pulpit, complete with tester, and a handsome vaulted chapel dating from the 15th century. The church was much

▲ *To reach Sellack Boat, the route crosses a graceful, single-span suspension bridge over the River Wye.*

restored during the 19th century.

A walk across riverside meadows leads to Sellack suspension footbridge **H**, built by public subscription in 1895. The site was once a ford and ferry crossing, and this is reflected in the name of the settlement on the other side, Sellack Boat.

The bridge is constructed of cast iron, steel and concrete, and crosses the river in a single graceful span of 190 feet (57m), the longest span of any bridge over the Wye. From its swaying deck, you can enjoy tranquil views of the river as it winds lazily around a loop called the Goose's Neck. Ahead, clearly visible on its hill, is the Church of St John the Baptist at King's Caple, and the end of the walk.

attractive in early spring.

The route follows a path marking the course of a minor road, Roman in origin, through Pengethley Park **E**. This National Trust property has massive oaks and overgrown fish ponds. Ahead is the Pengethley Manor Hotel, formerly a manor house. It was built in the 1820s to replace a Tudor mansion destroyed by fire. Adjoining the hotel is a garden centre offering refreshments.

RUINED MANSION

A ridge-top bridleway takes you to Caradoc **F**, an ancient camp associated with an ally of King Arthur. The Scudamore family built a mansion here in 1620, with grand oak-panelled rooms and fine decorated plasterwork. Tragically, this was destroyed in a disastrous fire in 1986. Beside the charred ruins are rows of stables housing racehorses. Throughout the course of the walk, you are likely to meet strings of these handsome animals prancing along the lanes or at full stretch along the practice gallops.

Below Caradoc is the village of Sellack, whose church **G** is the only one in England dedicated to St Tysilio. The Norman building enjoys

◄ *The Church of St Tysilio in Sellack, with its prominent 14th-century spire, sits in a pretty, walled churchyard.*

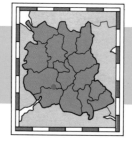

Climb to a hilltop viewpoint celebrated in a famous poem

▲ *The path from Elmley Castle up Bredon Hill offers fine views back to the lowlands. Hedge bindweed (inset), also known as bellbine or convolvulus, twines up shrubs on the route.*

This walk takes in one of the most celebrated views in southern or central England, so choose a fine day to be sure to see it at its best. The Clent and Lickey Hills lie due north; to the east is the long Cotswolds escarpment; the Severn and the Avon meander and gleam across ancient floodplains to the south and west, with the Malverns and the Forest of Dean beyond; Brown Clee and Abdon Burf stand out in the north-west, with The Wrekin in the far distance.

You start in the picturesque, thatched and half-timbered village of Elmley Castle Ⓐ. The name comes from the ancient manor of Elmley, a stretch of land cleared by Saxons around AD600, and a Norman keep. The overgrown remains of the castle overlook the village from Castle Hill. Its stones were plundered for garden walls, a bridge over the Avon, and extensions to the Church of St Mary's Ⓑ. The church has herring-bone patterned Saxon walls,

a Norman tower, a 13th-century font, superb carvings and sundials set into medieval crosses.

A pond and line of mature trees separate it from the castle's main contribution to the village; the deer park Ⓒ was enclosed in 1234 when Sir Walter Beauchamp received a gift of 10 does and three stags from the king. Their descendants can still be seen in the splendid parkland.

TOP OF THE WORLD

A long climb leads to the top of Bredon Hill Ⓓ. This strategic point was the junction of ancient track-ways and site of several fortresses. From its heights you can see eight old counties, and feel on top of everything for many miles around.

For many, its fame rests on *Bredon Hill*, a poem by A E Housman which captures the time-lessness of the place, from which the bells of 15 churches can be heard.

On the north-western edge of the hill is Kemerton Camp Ⓔ, a hill fort of around 200BC. Its row of double ditches crests the steep escarpment and encloses 22 acres (9 hectares).

Inside is a local landmark, the Banbury Stone Ⓕ. It is not a standing stone but a huge boulder of the Cotswold stone which covers the upper part of Bredon Hill. In the 18th century it stood near a cave. This was destroyed by a landslip, and the Banbury Stone split into several pieces. From one angle, it

ROGER VLITOS. INSET: TONY HARE

▼ *Parsons' Folly, once a summer-house, houses magnetic survey equipment.*

ROGER VLITOS

FACT FILE

☀ Elmley Castle, 6 miles (9.6km) south-west of Evesham, off the A44

▭ Pathfinders 1019 (SO 84/94) & 1042 (SO 83/93), grid reference SO 982411

miles 0 1 2 3 4 5 6 7 8 9 10 miles
kms 0 1 2 3 4 5 6 7 8 9 10 11 12 13 14 15 kms

◔ Allow 3 hours

▰ One long, steep ascent and descent. Well-signposted bridleways, footpaths and concessionary paths. Some sections of grazing land may be very muddy in wet weather. Walking boots recommended

P By village green

T Regular bus service from Evesham and Tewkesbury

▦ Old Mill Inn and The Queen Elizabeth, Elmley Castle

THE WALK

ELMLEY CASTLE – BREDON HILL

Start in the Square of Elmley Castle Ⓐ.

▶ Head south to St Mary's Church Ⓑ. Take the path from the corner of the graveyard, keeping the pond on your right. Cross two stiles and go along the field boundary and over a footbridge into the deer park Ⓒ, then make for a horse jump beneath large trees on its southernmost edge, passing below Castle Hill on your right. A footpath waymarked 'Wychavon Way' climbs steeply through aged woods to a field at the crest of Bredon Hill Ⓓ.

▶ Turn right, leaving the Wychavon Way, and follow a path on the edge of private woods on your right, to a five-bar gate.

▶ Go along a bridleway, with a fence on your left and open ground to your right, until you come to another gate with a copse of Scots pines on your left. Go through and continue straight along the crest to the ramparts of Kemerton Camp Ⓔ. Follow the path as it bears left past the Banbury Stone Ⓕ in the crater to the right of Parsons' Folly Ⓖ and left again along the ramparts of the camp entrance.

▶ Bear right to follow the track down and past a farm building. Turn left on another track, which is a concessionary path, and at the field edge go left again, heading back towards the gate beneath the copse of Scots pines.

▶ Turn right then follow the waymarked footpath as it descends along the line of the escarpment to your left, past the edge of the woodland and through another gate. Continue ahead down across scrubland to a hollow lane which leads down to Hill House Farm.

▶ Join a quiet country road and follow it downhill to the village. Cross the stile up the bank on the right, opposite two cottages almost at the bottom of the lane. A footpath diagonally left emerges by Manor Farm. Turn right to return to the main street and the square.

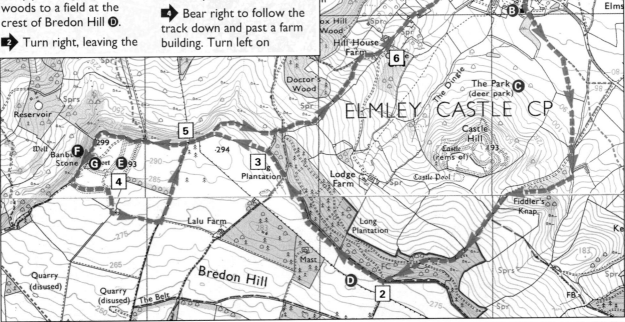

ROGER VLITOS

resembles a kneeling elephant, complete with tusks and trunk, and has been renamed 'the elephant stone'.

A charter dated AD779 mentions 'a city with the ancient name of Baenintes Burh' on top of the hill. By the time of the *Domesday Book* it had vanished, and there is no sign of it today. Quantities of imported iron ore have been found, which indicate a trading settlement, but there have been no archaeological excavations

◀ *These gilded tombstones, with children at their feet, are in St Mary's.*

beyond the Iron Age fort.

A stone tower within Kemerton Camp, known as 'Parsons' Folly' Ⓖ, was erected by a Mr Parsons as a summer-house with unbeatable views. As the hill here is 961 feet (293m) above sea-level, he built his tower to be 39 feet (12m) exactly, so the view from the roof would be from 1,000 feet (305m).

The route descends from here through fields and woods, with long views ahead over the fertile valley of the Avon, and your destination, Elmley Castle, in the foreground.

BLACK-AND-WHITE LANES

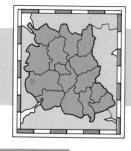

Splendid half-timbered houses set in a charming rural landscape

▲*Little Burton Farm, just north-east of Lower Burton, is one of many splendid half-timbered buildings in the area. The parasitic mistletoe (seen inset on an apple tree) grows in orchards nearby.*

This walk takes in the small market town of Pembridge and the village of Eardisland, at the northern edge of an area described by the architectural writer Alec Clifford-Taylor as 'unrivalled in England' for the quantity and quality of half-timbered, black-and-white buildings (see box on page 28).

Excellent examples can be found at the very start of the walk in the market place **Ⓐ** of Pembridge. The 16th-century market hall itself has had its upper storey removed, and retains its open ground stage, with eight carved posts supporting the roof. The handsome New Inn, to the north, is from the early 17th century, while the house at the south-west of the market place has parts that date to the 14th century.

You climb some ancient steps to St Mary's Church **Ⓑ**, which dates mostly from the 14th century, though it is a Norman foundation and the earthworks of a Norman castle can be found to the south. The spacious interior contains a 13th-century font, a Jacobean pulpit and some fine monuments, but the church's extraordinary feature is the detached belltower by the porch.

There are 40 such detached towers in England and Wales, and nine of them are in Herefordshire. The one at Pembridge is made of two stages of timber on a stone base. The massive 14th-century joinery of the structure can be appreciated from the walkway around the inside.

ALMSHOUSES

From the churchyard, you descend another set of old steps and pass the 16th-century Stores, with its fine oriel window, to enter Bridge Street. The Duppa Almshouses of 1661, one of two sets of black-and-white almshouses in the town, are at the

▶ *The belltower of St Mary's stands separate from the main church.*

RAY GRANGER. INSET: JEAN HALL/NATURE PHOTOGRAPHERS

FACT FILE

- ☀ Pembridge, 7 miles (11.2km) west of Leominster, on the A44

- 🗺 Pathfinders 993 (SO 25/35) and 994 (SO 45/55), grid reference SO 390581

  miles 0 1 2 3 4 5 6 7 8 9 10 miles
  kms 0 1 2 3 4 5 6 7 8 9 10 11 12 13 14 15 kms

- ◔ Allow 3½ hours

- ▬ Surfaced lanes almost all the way. No steep slopes. Mud and standing water on lanes make good walking shoes advisable

- **P** No official car parks. Room for cars around the market hall, on the village streets, or by the River Arrow

- **T** BR to Leominster. Buses are run by Primrose Motors, Tel. (01568) 612271

- ☕ The New Inn and the Red Lion in Pembridge; the Cross Inn and the White Swan in Eardisland

- 🍴 Eardisland Tea Rooms. Teas at Burton Court when open

- 🏰 Burton Court is open end May to end Sept, Wed–Thu, Sat–Sun, 2.30–6pm. Open to parties by arrangement. Tel. (01544) 388231. Admission charge

- **I** Tourist information at Eardisland Tea Rooms, Church Lane. Open daily, Tel. (01544) 388226

RAY GRANGER

THE WALK

PEMBRIDGE – EARDISLAND

*The walk begins at the market place **A**, just south of the main A44 road, in the centre of Pembridge.*

▶**1** Go up the steps to St Mary's Church **B**. Take the path that runs straight down to the left of the belltower. Go down the steps by the Stores, cross and walk along Bridge Street ahead. Continue across the River Arrow **C** to Clear Brook **D** on your right-hand side.

▶**2** Just beyond the house, turn right. Follow this winding lane all the way to The Green **E** in Eardisland.

▶**3** Turn left over the road-bridge, then immediately left again on a surfaced path beside the River Arrow. At the end, go over the stile ahead into the field containing Monk's Mound **F**. Continue along the left edge, and over the stile at the far end. Turn right along a cart track, to a surfaced road. Bear right to Staick House **G**. Cross the road, and turn right over the bridge. At the Cross Inn, turn left down Church Lane. Go through the lychgate, and right of the yew tree ahead to a metal gate. Follow the grassy path to a surfaced lane, and continue ahead to a kissing-gate. Follow the left-hand edge of the field ahead, through another kissing-gate. Where the fence turns left, go ahead and slightly right, past the corner of an orchard to a gate into the road.

▶**4** Turn left. After ½ mile (800m), you pass the entrance to Burton Court **H**. At the crossroads with the A44, cross with care and continue on the lane opposite. Ignore all turns off to the left.

▶**5** At a T-junction opposite a white bungalow, turn right. At the next T-junction, turn left. Turn left again at a T-junction opposite a house with a topiary yew in the front garden. Follow this lane to the next junction.

▶**6** Turn right. Follow this wider road, bearing right at a three-way junction, back to the market place.

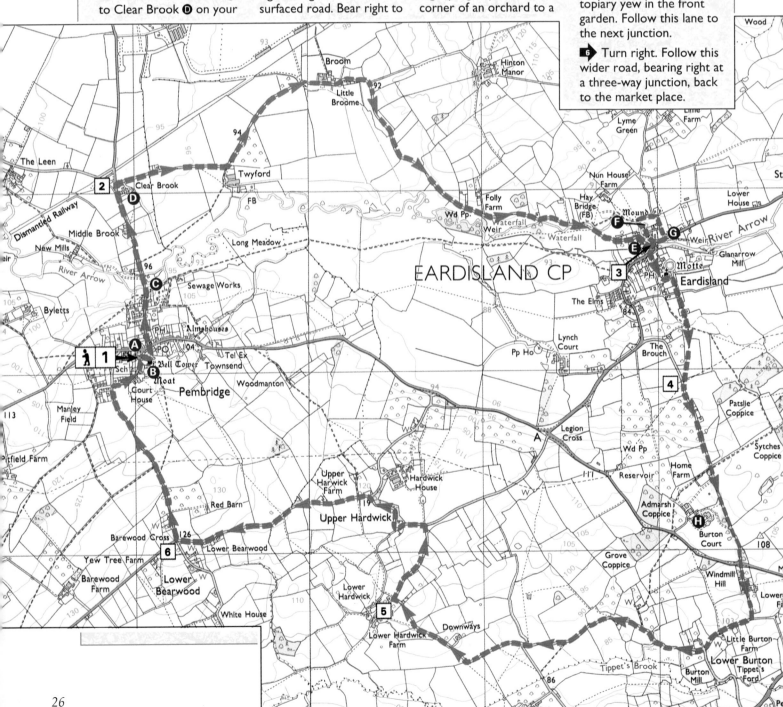

beginning of the street, while Glen Arrow cottages and Bridge Cottage, further down, are also worth a look.

A stone bridge takes you across the River Arrow **C**. The river rises in the Welsh mountains and joins the Lugg just south of Leominster. It meaders through a wide floodplain of lush meadows. A little way along the road is Clear Brook **D**. This large black-and-white house, with its three gables and its tall brick chimneys, dates from the 17th century.

You turn off down a lane bordered by hedges of hawthorn and holly, garlanded with berries in the autumn. Finches flit to and fro across the way, and, on both sides, pastures and arable fields stretch away towards distant hills. The illusion of timelessness is sometimes compromised — especially at weekends — by the light aircraft,

▲*At The Green at Eardisland, there is a good view of Arrow Cottage on the opposite bank of the river of the same name. Clear Brook (below) has fancy geometric designs in its gables.*

microlights and gliders taking off and landing at Shobdon Airfield, about a mile (1.6km) to the north.

The lane winds past an orchard of mature trees. The scents of blossom and fruit are overpowering in their seasons. The apples are used for cider-making, the closest thing the area has to an industry. Isolated farms have walls thickly covered in ivy that thrums with busy insects on warm late-summer days.

FOLLY FARM

Just past Folly Farm, the road runs along the Arrow; gaps in the hedge allow a glimpse of a weir. The sound of a small waterfall proves that the river's energy is not entirely spent.

Just past a tall, red-brick wall, you round a corner and come to a part of Eardisland known as The Green **E**. Fine houses line the grassy banks of the Arrow, which flows down towards a mellow stone

bridge. On the right is the pigeon house, a four-gabled, ivy-covered brick dovecote that is topped, rather incongruously, by a weathervane in the shape of a fish. This stands in the walled garden of the Manor House, a 17th-century, half-timbered house whose brick Queen Anne elevation faces the road.

The route crosses the bridge and goes back along the other side of The Green, into a field that contains the Monk's Mound **F**. This low, flower-covered earthwork, a circle some 30 yards (27m) in diameter, is of uncertain date and purpose.

A cart track and side road lead you back to the main street and Staick House **G**, the finest black-and-white building on the walk. Most of it dates from around 1300, though an east wing was added in the 17th century. The 14th-century hall still has a sandstone tile roof, and many of the original doors and windows are intact.

Across the road, the Arrow

▲*Apples from this orchard to the north-east of Pembridge are pressed to make the potent local cider.*

Nature Walk

The HONEY BEE and the COMMON WASP are common in orchards. The bee is attracted by pollen and nectar; wasps feed their young on aphids and caterpillars.

Black and White

There are two basic building styles in Britain: mass walling, where the weight is borne by solid supporting walls tied together with beams, and frame walling, where the load is transmitted to the ground via a rigid frame. Until the 20th century, this frame was invariably timber, and usually oak.

Often, the frame of posts, beams and braces was covered; tiles, shingles, weatherboarding, lath and plaster, and stucco were all hung from or fixed to the frames to weatherproof the walls. The alternative method was to leave the framework exposed, and to fill the gaps with wattle and daub or, more rarely, brick.

Smaller timbers called studs broke up the area to be filled into panels. Some studs and even supporting braces were carved into decorative shapes. Upright staves were slotted between the studs and interwoven with withies, to form the wattle; the daub, a mixture

The profusion of black-and-white, half-timbered houses on this walk is a good indicator that the area had great wealth towards the end of the Middle Ages.

including clay, horsehair, dung and straw, was slapped over this, inside and out, and the whole thing covered with coats of plaster.

In some areas, the oak was limed or allowed to weather to an iron-grey colour, and set off with colour washes over the plaster; in others, particularly in the Welsh Marches, Lancashire and the North Midlands, black timber and white plaster were favoured.

There were practical reasons for this; the timbers were coated in pitch and the panels in whitewash to protect them from rain. Illuminated manuscripts and paintings show that black-and-white buildings were already commonplace in the 15th century.

Although it is often identified as a Tudor style, timber-framing was the accepted method of building houses and other vernacular buildings over much of the country from around the 15th to the 18th century. The only exceptions were the occasional great house for a wealthy landowner, or the shanty hovels of the agricultural labourers.

The medieval black-and-white cottages that survive today were built originally as yeomen's houses. Where they survive in numbers, as in the countryside around Pembridge, Weobley and Eardisland, they indicate that the area prospered in the late Middle Ages.

ALL PHOTOS: RAY GRANGER

▲ *The 14th-century Staick House is festooned with attractive creeper.*

widens; between here and the bridge is a green bank where the village's varied population of ducks preens between clamouring for food. By the bridge is the old grammar school; one of its timbers was the village whipping post, and the manacles are still attached.

You leave the village via the churchyard. The church itself, another dedicated to St Mary, was

rather over-restored in 1864. From the yard's north-east corner, there are views over the mound and moat of a castle built here in Norman times to protect the river crossing.

A back road leads you to Burton Court ⓗ, a stone-built, 18th-century house whose Tudor-style front was designed by Williams-Ellis in 1912. The house incorporates a 14th-century hall, open to the roof, from an earlier, timber-framed building.

INFORMAL EXHIBITION

Burton Court is more a squire's house than a stately home, and is still lived in. It contains a fascinating exhibition of costume, with a whole room given over to oriental pieces, and various curios, including a model fairground and many stuffed and mounted animals. Part of the grounds are used for growing soft fruits; visitors may pick their own.

From here, the return route follows a lane past the half-timbered Little Burton Farm to a low, marshy

▶ *In the centre of Eardisland, the route crosses this finely proportioned stone bridge over the River Arrow.*

area of willows and dragonflies. The lane climbs very gently between tall, mature hedgerows. Views open out on either side, and you walk along the lanes through the hamlets of Upper and Lower Hardwick to a somewhat wider road, which returns you to Pembridge. If you have time, a stroll up and down the main street of this attractive town makes a pleasant end to the walk.

7

LITTLE EVEREST

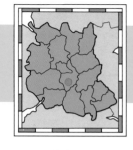

WARWICKSHIRE

◄*Pollarded trees surround the pool filled by a mineral spring, its health-giving properties now unused. Canada geese (inset), natives of America, at present number some 20,000 in Britain.*

From an attractive village to the highest point in Warwickshire

This walk climbs the highest hills in Warwickshire. The height reached is 850 feet (259 metres) and there are extensive views over the Avon vale. The uplands are of jurassic limestone and akin to the Cotswold escarpment. The scenery is similar and truly lovely with a combination of rough pasture sheeplands, woodlands teeming with wildlife, a great country mansion in a green hollow and a pretty village at the start.

The village is Ilmington, where the buildings are a mix of butter-hued limestone and weathered brick. (The name means 'elm grown

hill' but sadly that noble tree completely succumbed to Dutch elm disease a few years back.)

Ilmington has all the buildings typical of an English village. The village store seems to stock almost everything. There is a viable school. Old craftsmen such as the hurdle maker and potter survive. There are two historic inns and a catholic church but perhaps most splendid is St Mary's Church **A**. This church must be approached by footpaths and dates from the 13th century with magnificent Norman arches.

ELIZABETHAN MANOR

Nearby is Ilmington Manor **B**. This fine gabled house dates from Elizabethan times and was built with limestone from the local quarries, which were still worked until the 1920s. The house received some fame in 1934 when it was used in the first royal Christmas broadcast.

Another interesting building in Ilmington is the 17th-century Crab Mill House in Grump Street. Once this would have served the many cider orchards in the area.

From the church, you go through the churchyard and along pathways

PAUL FELIX. INSET E. K. THOMPSON/NATURE PHOTOGRAPHERS LTD

FACT FILE

- Ilmington, 8 miles (12.8 km) south of Stratford-on-Avon

- Pathfinders 1020 (SP 04/14) and 1021 (SP 24/34), grid reference SP 209434

| miles 0 | 1 | 2 | 3 | 4 | 5 | 6 | 7 | 8 | 9 | 10 miles |
| kms 0 | 1 | 2 | 3 | 4 | 5 | 6 | 7 | 8 | 9 | 10 11 12 13 14 15 kms |

- Allow 4 hours

- Some steep climbing. Tracks are usually well-drained but some parts very muddy in wet weather

- **P** Quiet streetside or Recreation Ground, Ilmington

- Red Lion and Howard Arms have bar food

PAUL FELIX

▲*The village of Ilmington is one of the prettiest in the county with mellow stone cottages and delightful gardens.*

THE WALK

ILMINGTON

The walk begins at the main gateway of St Mary's Church in Ilmington.

▶ **1** Start at the main gateway to the church **A**, which is on the same road as the school and The Hill Farm. Walk to the far corner of the churchyard and follow path and lane to Front Street. Nearby is Ilmington Manor **B** and the pound **C**.

▶ **2** Turn left a few steps. Opposite the Red Lion Inn turn right along the Shipston road then right again — the lane is signed to Compton Scorpion.

▶ **3** Follow the lane for about 1 mile (1.6 km). Opposite Southfield Farm take the cart track. Go through two gates and a little further on go through a gate which is just to the left of the track and leads to a pool **D** where wildfowl gather.

▶ **4** Turn right and cross the feeder brook at the far left corner of the field. In rough pastureland keep by the left-hand border and continue uphill to cross a stile onto a lane. Turn left into the lane and continue for about ½ mile (800 metres).

▶ **5** About 200 yards (180 metres) past some barns on the right-hand side, turn right down a cart track and proceed past a left-hand wood to a pasture. Cross to the far side and turn right, aiming towards the house of Foxcote **E**.

▶ **6** Go through a gate and along a tractor way. Within 100 yards (90 metres) take the path signed through the woods on your right.

▶ **7** Climb a stile out of the woods and turn left. Go through a gate to an area of grassland which may be enclosed by an electric fence. Take care as you crawl under the fence onto a drive. Bear left to pass in front of Foxcote alongside a left-hand hedge.

▶ **8** Keep ahead along main drive to pass a farmhouse on the right. Just beyond, take a bridleway — marked with a blue arrow — through a gate. Climb hillside to stepstile about halfway along top fence.

▶ **9** Follow clear way at the edge of fields, keeping sparse woodland to left. Continue to a lane. Turn right for 400 yards (360 metres). Opposite

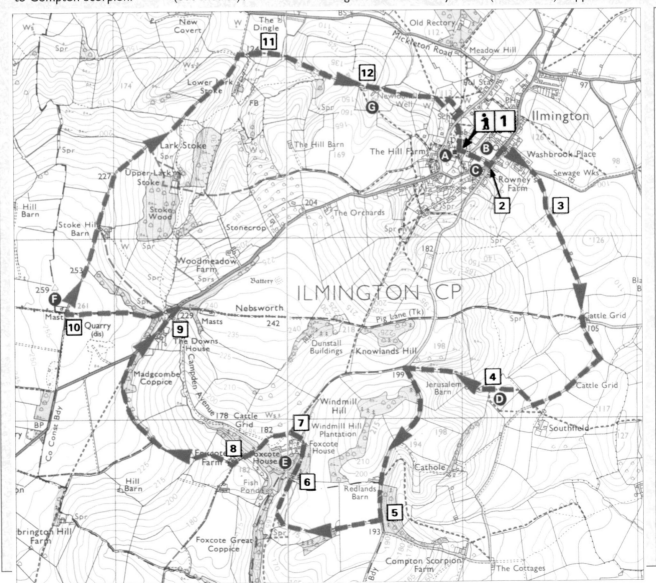

private drive to Foxcote go through gate on left. Pass to left of oak tree to bridlegate. Walk alongside stone wall to drover's road and highest point **F**. Here there is a radio transmitting station.

10 Turn right for I mile (1.6 km). By an old fallen tree turn right along farm drive. Keep the farmhouse on your right and continue straight on till you see the path signed ahead. Then go around edge of field and cross a stile to pasture.

11 Cross a brook then immediately bear left over another brook. Strike up the hillside (there is a waymark sign here) to a stile by a gate. Follow edges of fields.

12 Cross right-hand stile. Ignore the next stile (on right) and descend slope to chalybeate pool **G**. Climb the stile by the pool and continue over meadows, crossing three waymarked stiles which bring you to the back of the school. Go down path by side of school. Turn right into lane for a few paces, then cross to kissing gate. In pasture walk to far right corner to return to your starting point at Ilmington Church.

PAUL FELIX

▲*Formal topiary in the spring gardens of the gabled, 16th-century Ilmington Manor near the beginning of the walk.*

and a lane to Front Street by the village hall. Nearby stones in the grass indicate the area of the pound **C** where stray animals were penned.

Quiet lanes lead to a footpath, which passes by a newly constructed pool **D**. This has attracted many species of wildfowl — you may even see the elusive heron here. From the next footpath we overlook the gardens of Foxcote and soon see the early-Georgian house **E**.

Estate roads, which are public rights-of-way, lead to a path over sheeplands. The route continues to climb to the county's highest point — little Everest **F**. The high lane that you follow was once a Roman

AA PICTURE LIBRARY

▼*The tower of St Mary's Church can be seen in this view of Ilmington. The church is Norman, but the eleven wooden mouse carvings in the interior (above) are of a much later date.*

highway then a drover's road.

Past a farmstead a track is well waymarked to a pond filled by a chalybeate, or mineral, spring **G**, which for some years enjoyed a considerable vogue for its health-giving properties. As you descend you can see the ridge of Edge Hill (near the battle site of 1642) in the distance.

LOCAL FARMING

Within living memory Ilmington was a self-contained village with agriculture and service at the large houses providing the employment and a number of shops supplying the needs of the inhabitants. Farms were small and mainly sheep and dairy. In the 1890s a local carrier estimated that a ton of butter a week went to Stratford and in 1931 only ten per cent of the land was arable.

Nowadays only the hills are sheep pastures and the lower slopes are intensely sown, with barley and beans predominating. Oil seed rape (attractive when in flower but difficult for ramblers later in the season) is not cultivated hereabouts but a new crop is flax with its pretty pale blue flowers.

Few Ilmington residents work on the land; farms are family run with

JULIA PICKLES

outside contractors providing labour and machines when required. Sadly the intensification of farming has resulted in widespread destruction of hedgerows to create large, more easily worked fields.

There is a wide variety of wildlife to be observed on the ramble. Foxes are numerous and provide good sport for the hunt, which visits the area about twice a year. Rabbits are increasing in numbers and can cause widespread crop damage. There are badger sets on the route;

▲ The gracious, early-Georgian stone manor of Foxcote, set among surrounding hills, has a fine garden.

although you are unlikely to see these nocturnal creatures, there is much evidence of their presence.

With the many types of lowland, hill and water habitats you will see many species of birds. Along the lanes the hedgerows provide good cover for the common types but yellowhammers seem particularly prevalent. In the high woods game birds will scurry on your approach and the rooks find the tall trees to their liking for nest building.

BIRD LIFE

The route goes around several reed-fringed pools, which support coots, moorhens, ducks and Canada geese. More rare are the visiting heron and swans. The upland drover's road is through the area called Larkstoke. This is aptly named as, in spring and late summer, the trill of unseen larks is heard constantly.

The Ilmington Morris Men

The Ilmington Morris Men, perform a traditional dance to greet the dawn on their annual May Day performance.

Ilmington is the only village in Warwickshire where the 300-year-old tradition of Morris dancing is alive today. Two men played an important part in the maintenance of the tradition; they were Sam Bennet, known as the Ilmington fiddler from the late 1890s to his death in 1951, and Harry Sturch, also a fiddle player and a key figure in the revival of Morris dancing that took place after 1974.

The Ilmington Morris dancers are all men as Morris dancing is believed to be a traditional male fertility dance. The traditional dances they perform, specific to that village, number about 23 and include those such as the Broom dance and the Keeper (dedicated to the memory of Sam Bennet and danced to the old Warwickshire tune).

The dancers perform in their colours of gold and royal blue with two crossed ribbons over their shoulders. They wear grey top hats, white shirts and grey cord trousers adorned with bells and ribbons.

There are designated days when the Ilmington Morris Men can be seen performing. The most important is Gardens Day. This occurs one day in spring, when a dozen or so gardens in the village are open to the public. On May Day each year the Morris Men dance at dawn on Ilmington Down — the highest point in Warwickshire. They then perform outside Sam Bennet's old house and continue to perform through the village until 8 am.

Each Boxing Day, dances are performed in neighbouring Shepston-on-Stour in old people's homes and hospitals. The significance of this day is that Cecil Sharp, an academic who collected Morris dances around the country, had his interest in this custom aroused when he saw a performance on Boxing Day in 1899 at Headington Quarry in Oxford.

▲ The gentle rolling scenery of the Warwickshire countryside before the ascent to the county's highest point.

MIDLAND WATERWAYS

8

WARWICKSHIRE

From a peaceful hillside village through quiet farmlands

The village of Napton, where the walk begins, is very much 'on the hill', standing high above the surrounding countryside. From the village there is a short stroll across fields to a lane that leads down to the valley. Part-way down there is a splendid view of the locks **A** on the Oxford Canal and of the tower windmill —a prominent landmark at the top of the hill. Further down are flooded clay pits, the clay being used for brick-making. By the canal are the old stables, reminders that once the working boats on the canal were all pulled by horses.

BRINDLEY'S CANAL

The next section of the walk follows the towpath. Building the canal started in 1769 and James Brindley, the chief engineer, followed his usual practice of running it along the natural contours of the land, so that it snakes its way around the hill. The towpath is narrow and often overgrown in summer, so walkers have to move in single file. It is a delight for lovers of wild flowers: on one side you have a range of hedgerow plants; on the other the reeds and water plants.

ROBERT EAMES. INSET: A. CHRISTIANSEN/FRANK LANE PICTURE AGENCY

FACT FILE

Napton on the Hill, 3 miles (5 km) east of Southam

Pathfinder 977 (SP 46/56), grid reference SP 463611

miles 0 1 2 3 4 5 6 7 8 9 10 miles
kms 0 1 2 3 4 5 6 7 8 9 10 11 12 13 14 15 kms

3½ to 4 hours

Easy going, but the towpath is narrow and overgrown

P Napton on the Hill, by the triangular green in the centre

Napton, also at Napton Bridge on the A425

There are still reminders of the old life of the canal. The first road bridge has been widened to allow for modern traffic, but you can still see how the original bridge was built on the skew, involving a complex pattern of bricklaying. Beyond it is a widened section of canal known as a winding hole, where the 70-foot- (21-metre-) long old working narrow-boats could be turned.

WIDE LOCKS

The walk now leaves the canal and continues across fields to Napton Reservoirs **B**. These were built to supply water for the canal and are now very popular with water birds of all kinds. Beyond is another canal, the Grand Union, which was built later than the Oxford. It has wide locks able to take two narrowboats, side by side. You continue across fields and by an area of woodland, before rejoining the Oxford Canal by a dismantled bridge.

▲*A view of Napton Locks, a series of nine narrow locks where the Oxford Canal drops to the junction with the Grand Union Canal. A female mallard (inset).*

Leaving the canal, the walk goes past the curious little gothic church of Lower Shuckburgh. The interior is even more remarkable than the exterior, with bright red brick pillars and arches. The path now leads steadily up the grassy hill towards a knoll crowned with trees. It runs close to a large private wood on one side, with an attractive lake, surrounded by rhododendra; while to the left one sees Shuckburgh Park, with its little chapel and home farm.

The route now runs along the ridge of the hills and from the

THE WALK

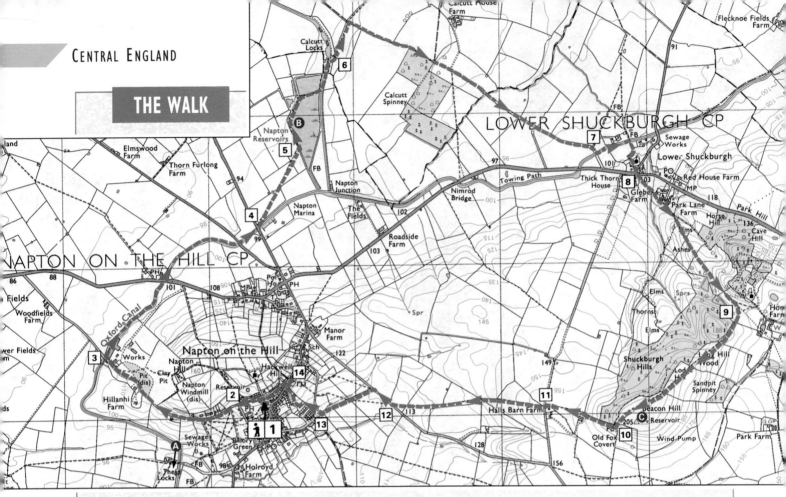

NAPTON ON THE HILL – UPPER SHUCKBURGH – LOWER SHUCKBURGH

The walk starts at the triangular green in the centre of Napton on the Hill.

1 With your back to the Crown Inn, take the footpath to the left, past the thatched cottage. Take the path alongside the boundary of the cottage (that may be extremely overgrown), cross the stile and head over the field to the roadway where you turn right.

2 At the road junction turn left past the view of Napton Locks **A** to the canal.

3 Cross the bridge over the canal, turn right to join the towpath, then left onto the towpath — away from, not under, the bridge.

4 Leave the towpath by turning left just before the bridge at Napton Marina. Cross the road to the stile, and take the footpath diagonally across to the opposite corner.

5 Take the path up to Napton Reservoirs' **B** bank, turn left and follow the path round to the right across the bridge. At the canal turn left. Cross the canal at the lock.

6 Go through the gap in the hedge by the bottom lock gates, through the iron gate and turn left to follow the line of the hedge to the gate. Beyond the gate turn right to follow the path along the edge of the field and past the small wood.

7 Where the track swings left, carry straight on up the little rise, and go down the bank to join the towpath. Turn left and leave the towpath to cross the canal on the iron footbridge, then follow the fence round to the gate at the right of the church.

8 Cross the main road and turn left. Cross the stile beside the stone cottage, and take the footpath across the fields towards the farm building. The path across the fields is waymarked by yellow arrows towards the hill crowned by woodland.

9 Where the path divides near the top of the hill, continue on along the edge of the woodland, over the top of Beacon Hill **C**.

10 At the edge of the woodland, follow the track round to the right and head downhill towards the brick barns. The path has been routed to cut across the corner of the field and then follows the edge of the field to protect crops.

11 At the roadway, turn left, then immediately right on the far side of the fence. Watch out for a gap in the fence where the path cuts to the right across the field and to a stile. The path continues over stiles to the road.

12 At the road turn right. At the road junction turn left, signposted to Napton.

13 At next junction turn right up Godsons Lane.

14 At the main road, turn left to return to the start.

summit **C** there are wide views of the countryside. Napton Hill can be seen, as can two more modern structures: the tall telecommunications tower and the complex of masts that marks the radio station at Daventry, to the east. Nearer at hand, there is a 'fossilized' medieval farming landscape, the old pattern of ridge and furrow formed by the plough still visible under the grass.

The path now leads back down-hill to the farmland of the valley, where it skirts round, and at times cuts through, fields of grain. The walk is completed on the roads leading back to Napton, including a steep climb up Godsons Lane.

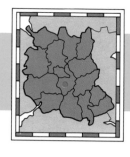

From historic Alcester along a Roman road and through woodland

The walk sets out from the historic town of Alcester and takes in part of Ryknild Street, a great Roman highway that ran from Wall, near Lichfield, in Staffordshire to Stow-on-the-Wold in Gloucestershire, where it met the Fosse Way. Next, the route leads through the tiny hamlets of Wixford and Exhall, with their wealth of timber-framed, black-and-white buildings and returns to Alcester via a path along the borders of the Forestry Commission's Oversley Wood. There are many deciduous trees here, and in autumn they form a rich, colourful backdrop.

A variety of wildlife may be encountered in the small area covered by this walk. There is much evidence — especially along Ryknild Street — of a rapidly increasing rabbit population. You may also see signs of badgers here — though you are far more likely to spot their setts, slides and dung pits than the animals themselves.

There have been many Roman finds in Alcester **A**, several of them in recent years, when new buildings were being constructed. Many of Alcester's ancient buildings have been carefully renovated. Malt Mill Lane, in particular, is lined with magnificent rows of medieval timber-framed houses with projecting upper storeys. Its restoration has won several architectural awards.

Nearby is the early 17th-century town hall, which once had open arches and a covered market place below. Dominating the town centre is the tower of the parish church, much of which was rebuilt in 1730 after a disastrous fire.

As you walk along Ryknild Street **B**, you can catch glimpses of the

◀ *Malt Mill Lane in Alcester has some finely-preserved, half-timbered Tudor buildings. Just north of Exhall there are woods containing coppiced beech trees (below left) like these.*

JANET HARRISON/AQUILA. INSET: E.A. JANES/NHPA

hamlet of Arrow, named after the river. Its church is notable for its tower, said to have been designed by Horace Walpole. Further downstream is Arrow Mill **C**, which was still grinding corn in the 1970s. It is now an hotel, and the turning mill wheel is a feature of the restaurant.

CAPABILITY BROWN

In front of the mill is a motte, or mound **D**, on which a wooden castle, built by Robert le Boteler in the 12th century, once stood. Nothing remains of it today. Beyond it, on a distant, wooded hillside, stands the grand mansion of Ragley Hall **E**, the home of the Marquis of Hertford. Its impressive grounds were laid out in the 1750s by Capability Brown.

St Milburga's Church **F** in Wixford has a timber-framed bell turret and contains some fine 15th-century brasses depicting Thomas de Crewe, who was a lawyer and

FACT FILE

✳	Alcester, 7 miles (11km) west of Stratford-upon-Avon
▱	Pathfinder 997 (SP 05/15), grid reference SP 089573

miles 0 1 2 3 4 5 6 7 8 9 10 miles
kms 0 1 2 3 4 5 6 7 8 9 10 11 12 13 14 15 kms

◔	Allow 3 hours
◼	Lowland farmland and deciduous woods. Several small hills. Paths are clear and well trodden, although some can be muddy in winter. Beware of nettles
P	Several off-street car parks in Alcester
🍴📷	Inns, hotels and cafés in Alcester. Two inns in Wixford
T	Stratford Road, Alcester
🏰	St Milburga's Church, Wixford

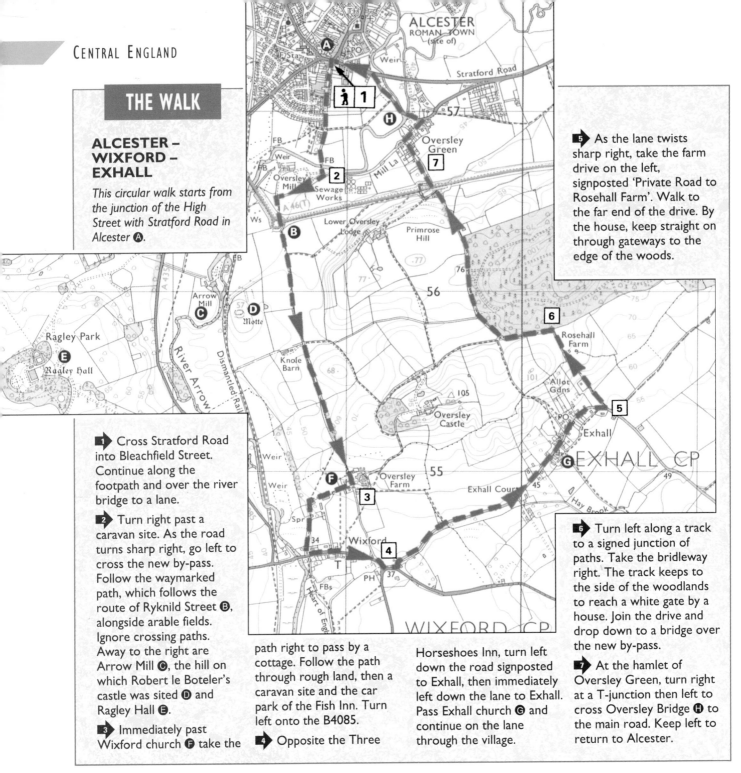

THE WALK

ALCESTER – WIXFORD – EXHALL

This circular walk starts from the junction of the High Street with Stratford Road in Alcester Ⓐ.

1 Cross Stratford Road into Bleachfield Street. Continue along the footpath and over the river bridge to a lane.

2 Turn right past a caravan site. As the road turns sharp right, go left to cross the new by-pass. Follow the waymarked path, which follows the route of Ryknild Street Ⓑ, alongside arable fields. Ignore crossing paths. Away to the right are Arrow Mill Ⓒ, the hill on which Robert le Boteler's castle was sited Ⓓ and Ragley Hall Ⓔ.

3 Immediately past Wixford church Ⓕ take the path right to pass by a cottage. Follow the path through rough land, then a caravan site and the car park of the Fish Inn. Turn left onto the B4085.

4 Opposite the Three Horseshoes Inn, turn left down the road signposted to Exhall, then immediately left down the lane to Exhall. Pass Exhall church Ⓖ and continue on the lane through the village.

5 As the lane twists sharp right, take the farm drive on the left, signposted 'Private Road to Rosehall Farm'. Walk to the far end of the drive. By the house, keep straight on through gateways to the edge of the woods.

6 Turn left along a track to a signed junction of paths. Take the bridleway right. The track keeps to the side of the woodlands to reach a white gate by a house. Join the drive and drop down to a bridge over the new by-pass.

7 At the hamlet of Oversley Green, turn right at a T-junction then left to cross Oversley Bridge Ⓗ to the main road. Keep left to return to Alcester.

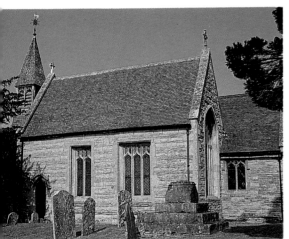

advisor to Margaret Beauchamp, Countess of Warwick, and his wife. The brasses are over 9 feet (3m) long. The church is sometimes locked but a key is available.

To the east is Exhall, a hamlet reputed to be one of the 'Shakespearean villages', visited by the bard and his companions for drinking contests. Its church Ⓖ includes some Norman work. The woods beyond Exhall have an abundance

◀ *In the graveyard of St Milburga's Church stands the weatherbeaten plinth of an ancient stone cross.*

of bird life and wild produce; in autumn, there are elderberries, crab apples, hazel nuts, sloes and black-berries. Note also the coppiced trees — beeches were regularly cut near to the ground to provide a crop of poles for making sheep hurdles.

The route drops down to the valley again to cross the River Arrow via Oversley Bridge Ⓗ, a six-arched structure built in 1600. As you cross the river, you may see mallard, Canada geese, moorhens and even a kingfisher. There are water voles here, too, though they scurry for cover if they are alarmed.

THE FOREST OF ARDEN

Mellow countryside and a towpath walk in the heart of England

The small town of Henley-in-Arden **A**, the starting point for this walk, is a pretty town whose long High Street is a living museum of English vernacular architecture. Medieval cottages rub eaves and gables with well-restored yeoman's houses and ancient coaching inns.

The walk starts by the 15th-century Church of St John, which juts resolutely into the main street, and continues down a lane to the Norman Beaudesert Church **B**. This was the original parish church, but was replaced by St John's because the River Alne often flooded in wintertime, cutting the parishioners off from their place of worship.

DE MONTFORT CASTLE

A little further on is a hill **C** that was the site of an 11th-century castle, the seat of the de Montfort family. The fortunes of the castle declined after the lord of the manor, Peter, was slain with his kinsman, Simon de Montfort, at the Battle of Evesham in 1265. Little remains today.

Rabbits burrow in the soft soil of the hill, which gives long views over the flat lands which once formed the vast Forest of Arden. Small pockets of the ancient woodland still remain.

▲Black-and-white timber-framed cottages in Henley-in-Arden's High Street make a charming starting point to the walk. Tench (inset) thrive in the slow-moving River Alne.

THE WALK

- Henley-in-Arden, 15 miles (24km) south of Birmingham on the A34

- Pathfinder 975 (SP 06/16), grid reference SP 151660

  miles 0 1 2 3 4 5 6 7 8 9 10 miles
  kms 0 1 2 3 4 5 6 7 8 9 10 11 12 13 14 15 kms

- 2½ hours

- Gently undulating countryside. Mix of pasture, woodland, roads and canal towpath. Some of the paths are not well-used, but the route is clear

- P On street or in car parks in Henley

- Pubs and restaurants in Henley-in-Arden and Preston Bagot

◀The steeply pitched roof of disused Blackford Mill indicates that it was probably once crowned with thatch.

The walk continues through farmland to the scattered hamlet of Preston Bagot, with its fine hilltop church **D**. It then drops down to the valley of a fast-flowing brook and follows the towpath of the Stratford-upon-Avon Canal.

RESTORED CANAL

The canal was built between 1793 and 1816 to join the Grand Union Canal with the Worcester and Birmingham Canal. The longboats carried mostly coal on the south-bound journey and returned laden with wheat and lime.

Trade dropped off at the end of the 19th century and the waterway was derelict for many years. It came

THE WALK

HENLEY-IN-ARDEN – PRESTON BAGOT

The walk begins in Henley High Street Ⓐ.

1 ▶ Walk along Beaudesert Lane beside St John's Church. Cross the River Alne and continue past the Church of St Nicholas Ⓑ. As the lane twists sharp right, keep ahead to pass through the kissing gate.

2 ▶ Take the direction indicated by the waymark arrow to go over the hill Ⓒ on which the de Montfort castle was situated. Keep along the clear path to climb a ridge where there are two step stiles. Climb the right-hand one to enter a pasture.

3 ▶ Walk just to the right of the electricity line to a stile into a lane. Turn left and follow the lane to Kate's Cottage. Go through the metal gate on the right and keep to the hedge on the left. Before the end of the field, go through a green metal gate.

4 ▶ Cross the field, aiming to the right of the farmstead. Go over a waymarked stile, then over another stile by a barn. Cross the lane to continue on the path opposite, up the hill and past Preston Bagot church Ⓓ to a lane. Cross a marked fence stile to a path.

5 ▶ Descend through a

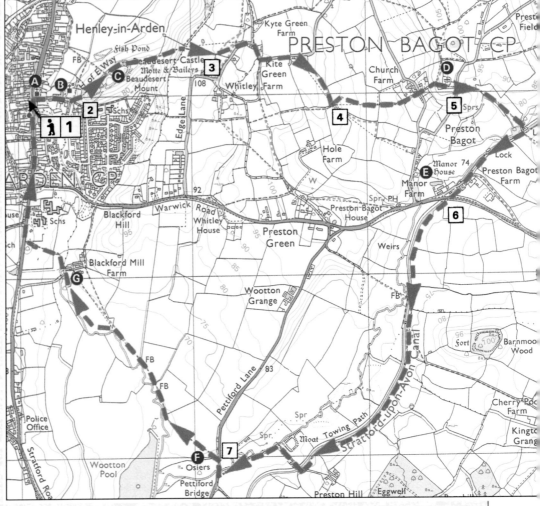

pasture and walk to the end of the next field. Cross the bridge and go past the tea rooms, then go over a lane to the canalside. Cross the water and turn right along the towpath. Preston Bagot Manor House Ⓔ is on your right just before you go under the B4095.

6 ▶ Continue along the

canal for 1¼ miles (2km). Turn right along a tarmac farm drive over a bridge and pass the field with the moated house outline. Turn right on the road alongside the osier beds Ⓕ.

7 ▶ Climb a stile to the meadow on the left. Walk diagonally across to the far side and go over another

stile by the river. Turn right and keep near to the river to Blackford Mill Ⓖ. Turn left along the drive, then immediately right over the weir. Follow the path to the playing field. Bear slightly right to the main road, where you turn right to return to Henley and the starting point.

---

into the hands of the National Trust, and after restoration by enthusiastic bands of volunteers, it reopened to traffic in 1964. It is now busy with pleasure boats in the summer.

Among the features to look out for on the way are bridges with slits down the middle so that the towing horses did not have to be unhitched, and lock-keepers' cottages with distinctive barrel roofs, perhaps adapted from templates for bridges.

Not long after joining the towpath, you will see a restored, timber-framed manor house Ⓔ on the other side of the water.

OSIER BEDS

After leaving the waterway, the route crosses pasture and meadowland and then briefly joins a road past some osier beds Ⓕ, where willow trees were regularly coppiced to provide the raw material

for wicker basketmakers.

The final part of the walk follows the course of the River Alne. The pools of this meandering stream are home to ducks and swans and increasingly large flocks of Canada geese, which are becoming a problem to neighbouring farmers.

From Blackford Mill Farm Ⓖ, where flour was ground from local crops for centuries, it is just a short walk back along a road to Henley.

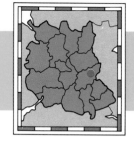
Follow a quiet flowing river from a Georgian market town

Oundle is an idyllic English country town. Sheltered on three sides in a wide loop of the river Nene, it stands on the site of a 7th-century monastery founded by St Wilfred. A place of pilgrimage and a prosperous market in late Saxon times, Oundle today is one of the most attractive Georgian towns in the country.

The main street is bordered by tall, dignified houses ranging over three centuries, displaying an interesting array of historical architectural features including gables, oriels and dormers.

The walk along the banks of the Nene is easy and relaxing, but an initial short itinerary around the centre of the town is time well spent. The lettered street plan is designed to indicate some of the more noteworthy buildings that could be seen in the course of a short visit.

The Talbot Hotel **Ⓐ**, which was rebuilt in 1826, has a fine carriage door matched by a round-arched window of the central bay, and flanked on either side by handsome bay windows in both storeys. The

▲ *Oundle is bordered on three sides by the River Nene. Swans and Canada geese can be seen and, in summer, the green-veined white butterfly (inset).*

Talbot is beyond doubt one of the oldest inns in the country. Inside some features of an earlier building have survived, notably the medieval timber-framed back range with what was once an open gallery.

Cobthorne House **Ⓑ** is an eye-catching building of unusual quality — even the adjoining barn has a stone mullion window in the gable. Cobthorne was built in 1656 for Major General William Butler, a close associate of the Lord Protector, Oliver Cromwell, and a member of the Council of State in the Instrument of Government.

WAR MEMORIAL

Oundle School Chapel **Ⓒ** was built in 1922 as a memorial to the school's dead in World War I. The east window was designed by John Piper in richly coloured glass.

St Peter's Church **Ⓓ** stands in a large, quiet churchyard well away from the busy market place. The tall, slender tower with its graceful lancet windows and elegant bell-openings is truly a masterpiece of English Decorated architecture.

In the south-east corner of the churchyard is Laxton School **Ⓔ**. This replaced the old school, originally the guild hall. The school was rebuilt in Tudor style in 1855.

Latham's Hospital **Ⓕ** is a relic of the early-17th century. It has three gables with decorated points and two courtyards with gates surmounted by a cross and a pelican, the latter is a symbol of compassion.

Ashton **Ⓖ** is an attractive estate village of early-20th-century thatched cottages where the inn, the Chequered Skipper, was named after a local butterfly now extinct.

▼ *Oundle School Chapel contains seven stained glass windows showing Shakespeare's Seven Ages of Man.*

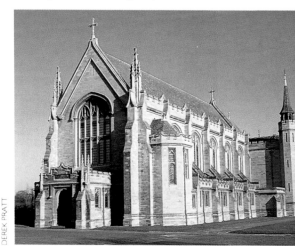

FACT FILE

✳ Oundle, 9 miles (14.4 km) east of Corby, 13 miles (20.8 km) south-west of Peterborough

🚏 Pathfinder 939 TL 08/18, grid reference TL 042880

miles 0   1   2   3   4   5   6   7   8   9   10 miles
kms 0 1 2 3 4 5 6 7 8 9 10 11 12 13 14 15 kms

🕐 Allow 2 hours

▬ Fairly level, clearly marked footpath along river bank. One short stretch of arable land could be muddy in wet weather

🅿 Free public car park and public toilets in St Osyth's Lane

🏨 Hotels, inns and cafés in Oundle

THE WALK

OUNDLE – NENE WAY

The walk begins at the car park in St Osyth's Lane in the centre of Oundle.

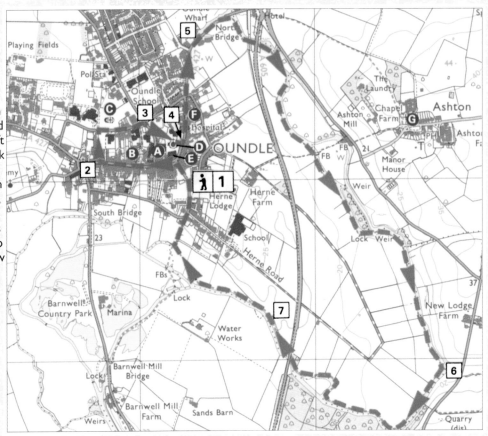

1 From the free car park in St Osyth's Lane turn right and after 50 yards (45 metres) left into the Market Place, to walk right of the Town Hall, which was built in the Tudor style in 1826. Go along the delightful, unexpected Doric colonnade of the School Bookshop. This structure was neatly added to a 17th-century house to allow the upper storey to expand over the pavement. Continue along the Market Place until you come to New Street and almost behind the war memorial find the Talbot Hotel **A**. Cross over New Street and the road now becomes West Street. On the right-hand side the handsome house that stands back from the street is Cobthorne House **B**, the home of the headmaster of Oundle School. Further down West Street, on the right-hand side, are two houses with fine bays linked by a high wall with an Elizabethan gateway.

2 Close by on the same side, opposite the Manor House, turn up a narrow unmarked lane, Inkerman Way, follow it past the Music School and go through a white gate. Now walk along a gravelled path going left then right to come out on Milton Road. Opposite is Oundle School Chapel **C** in the midst of well-kept lawns. Turn right into Milton Road, continuing to the crossroads.

3 At the crossroads turn right and carry on down New Street. Enter the church-yard on the left side of the road to reach St Peter's Church **D** and Laxton School **E**.

4 Now turn left along North Street, noting the White Lion with its three gables. Built in 1641, it served for many years as an inn and is now used by the School. About 50 yards (45 metres) along North Street come to Latham's Hospital **F** then continue to Station Road. Go past the Oundle Town football ground and continue walking out of town. Just before you cross the long bridge over the Nene take the footpath on the right leading down to the river.

5 The river walk is part of the popular Nene Way and is well waymarked throughout with the familiar black arrow on a white circle. Over the stile the path goes across sheep pasture, under the by-pass and along the bank of the quiet-flowing river. The by-pass, which has been such a boon to the town in removing heavy traffic from the narrow streets, rather spoils the first stage of the walk with intrusive noise, but as the river meanders away from the road peace and quiet return. Soon pass a metal bridge over the river and get a glimpse of the village of Ashton **G** near the opposite bank. Tall, ancient willows now line that bank and on your side the meadows are adorned with teasel, purple loosestrife and ragwort. Follow the riverbank through more sheepland and, as the river moves away from the by-pass, the walk becomes more serene, offering delightful views across the rich Northamptonshire countryside. There are more stiles and meadows as the path follows the river making a right-angle bend to the right.

6 Over yet another stile enter a large arable field where the farmer has left a good headland. The footing could be quite muddy in wet weather. Ahead now is a splendid view with the graceful top and spire of St Peter's church standing out on the skyline. Over another stile the path goes under the by-pass once more and then winds through rough spinney to rejoin the river where the bank is thick with teasels and flowering reeds.

7 Now there is another short stretch of sheepland and then the path turns half-right across the pasture with several attractive, detached modern houses away on the right. Over a tall stile near a metal gate at the top of the lane turn right into St Osyth's lane and the car park.

DEENE PARK

◀*Deene Hall, in its elegant lakeside setting, is largely 16th century. The extensive park has a formal garden. Less formal is black bryony (inset), a common hedgerow climbing plant.*

Rose Cottage in the village. The main features of interest are the ornate chancel with its brightly painted walls and barrel roof, and the splendid Brudenell monuments which are in a gated chapel in the south aisle. Lady Adeline Cardigan engaged the German sculptor Johann Erasmus Boehm to produce, in fine white marble, two life-sized recumbent effigies: one of Lord Cardigan and one of herself. Round the sides of the tomb are carved scenes of his exploits in the Crimean War. At the four corners are four bronze seahorses.

The road that leads from Deene Hall to Kirby Hall **C** is edged with

PAUL FELIX. INSET: BOB GIBBON

Stately homes and formal gardens

This peaceful ramble crosses open parkland and goes along quiet lanes above the valley of Willow Brook. The walk starts in the tiny, unspoilt limestone village of Deene that lies in the trees along the northern edge of Deene Park.

In a county renowned for its fine country houses it would be difficult to find one to surpass Deene Hall **B** for the serene beauty of its setting and the splendour of its gardens which make superb use of the lakes formed by the damming of Willow Brook. The garden is noted for its rare shrubs and old-fashioned roses.

The beautiful house has been the

home of the Brudenell family since 1514. In 1663 Sir Thomas Brudenell, great grandson of Robert, Henry VIII's Chief Justice, was created first Earl of Cardigan as a reward for his loyalty to the royalist cause during the Civil War and founded the family fortune.

The most famous of the Brudenells, however, was James Thomas, seventh Earl of Cardigan who was born 26th October, 1797. On October 25th 1854 he led the Charge of the Light Brigade at Balaclava, against the Russians, during the Crimean War. Less than 200 of the 675-strong brigade survived and 475 horses were slaughtered.

MEMENTOS OF WAR

This heroic, but tactically misguided, assault was immortalized by Tennyson in his poem *The Charge of the Light Brigade*. Numerous portraits and mementos of Lord Cardigan and this event are to be found at Deene Park.

The 13th-century church of St Peter **A** in Deene Park was restored by Lord Cardigan's widow in the late 1860s and dedicated to his memory. The key is available at

FACT FILE

⚹ Deene Park, off the A43, 7 miles (11.2 km) north-east of Corby

▭S Pathfinder 917 (SP 89/99), grid reference SP 951927

miles 0 1 2 3 4 5 6 7 8 9 10 miles
kms 0 1 2 3 4 5 6 7 8 9 10 11 12 13 14 15 kms

◔ Allow 1½ hours for walk; 1½ hours for the Hall and Church

▬ Not suitable for very young children or pushchairs. Trousers are recommended

P In lay-by near entrance to Deene Church

🍴 Both Deene Hall and Kirby Hall provide light refreshments

🏰 Deene Hall: open to public 2.00pm–5.00pm on Sunday and Monday of Bank Holiday weekends; also open Sunday from 1 June to 31 August. At other times viewing by private arrangement with Estate Office. Kirby Hall: open to the public all year round from 10.00am to 1.00pm and from 2.00pm to 6.00pm.

THE WALK

DEENE

The walk begins at a lay-by near the path leading to Deene Church Ⓐ.

▶ From the lay-by turn left up the village street past the entrance to Deene Hall Ⓑ, passing the old school on the right and the mossy-thatched Blacksmiths' Cottage on the left. The road climbs and wanders right, left, then right again past farm buildings.

▶ At a T-junction turn left along the road signposted Kirby Hall 1¼ miles (2 km). This quiet road runs above the valley of Willow Brook and offers bracing views across arable fields and parkland with distant woodlands. The road passes the end of a long plantation of firs, goes left past a fine stand of poplars and left again to give the first view of Kirby Hall Ⓒ nestling in the valley of Gretton Brook. Continue along the quiet, tree-lined road to reach the entrance to Kirby Hall.

▶ Opposite the entrance to the Hall go through a gate (this may be closed and will need to be climbed over) and walk along a grass track for about 100 yards (90 metres).

▶ Go left where a track comes in from the right. The path runs between the remains of ancient hawthorn hedges on either side. Go over a broken stile at a wire fence. Cross a tiny spinney, being careful of nettles; keeping on the same heading, go over a wide, rough pasture, staying parallel with the road on the left and the wood on the right. (This is a favourite haunt of skylarks and the air is filled with their thrilling songs.) Aim for a tall, flat-topped Scots pine in the wood ahead. Keeping left of the pine, cross a grassy track and, keeping on the same heading, go through a short stretch of wood to find a tall post at the edge of an arable field. Follow the line of white-topped posts in the field. Go through a green metal gate and cross the park, keeping on the familiar heading, to pass the farm buildings on the left and the lake on the right.

▶ At the farm track turn left over the cattle grid and follow the farm lane back into the village, then turn right to return to the start.

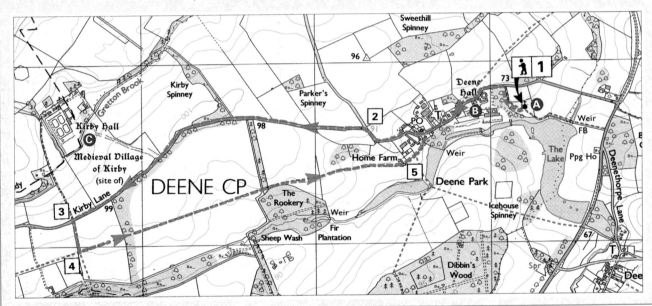

wide grass verges. These are relics of enclosure days when they were left for drovers to graze their cattle and sheep on the way to market. Today they are ideal picnic sites and, more importantly, they allow space for cow parsley, rough chervil, red and white campion, dead nettle and the modest dog's mercury.

Kirby Hall is worth a short detour as it is one of the most beautiful Elizabethan buildings in the country and demonstrates the extent to which classical influences were affecting the ornament and planning of English buildings in the late Elizabethan period. The formal gardens of the hall were laid out in approximately 1685 and have undergone a complete restoration.

◀ *The Church of St Peter is originally 13th century, though restored in the 19th century. Kirby Hall (right), an uninhabited ruin, is an important example of Elizabethan architecture.*

BOTH PHOTOS: PAUL FELIX

Over the crest of the rise, you descend to the Charwelton road. The valley ahead is occupied by the superbly clear earthworks of the deserted medieval village of Charwelton **E**, the houses of which were cleared away by the early 16th century, at the behest of three generations of the Andrewes family. A former road, or hollow way, runs from left to right, with remains of house platforms on either side.

The Church of the Holy Trinity **F** has a collection of monuments to the Andrewes family. The porch has a low, stone, rib-vaulted roof and its archway frames a good view of the deserted village site. Charwelton House, opposite, was built after the village was abandoned. This four-square, hipped-roof, ironstone house dates from the early 18th century.

WILDFOWL PONDS

The route continues parallel to a spectacular system of ponds and islets **G** described on the 1847 tithe map as fish-ponds, but more likely to have been provided for wildfowl.

You cross a dismantled railway into modern-day Charwelton **H**, with cottages along the lane and a village green. At the end, the pavement crosses a narrow, two-arched, late medieval packhorse bridge **J**. The route back to the start passes Charwelton Hall **K**, an ironstone Georgian house with coped gables.

▼*An elaborate memorial to several Knightleys, including Sir Richard (died 1534), who was the first to be knighted.*

▲*Fawsley Hall, the home of the Knightley family for 300 years, was derelict by the 1970s, but has been restored. Bulbous buttercups (left) dot the grasslands of the park.*

Visit a great estate and the remains of a medieval village

This walk explores the effect the enclosures of the 15th century had on the landscape and those who lived in it. It begins by a dry valley whose slopes are corrugated with ridges and furrows. These ripples are a hallmark of the rural Midlands; they are the pattern of the 15th-century village fields that were swept away when enclosures turned the area into a huge sheep run.

You pass Fawsley Farm **A**, an 18th-century house in the local limestone, on the way to Fawsley Hall **B**. This was the home of the Knightley family, lords of the manor here for several centuries, who were responsible for the local enclosures. It is set in parkland laid out by Capability Brown, much of which has reverted to farmland, though Brown's ornamental lakes survive as a reminder of its former splendour.

The walk goes through the park to the church **C**, which is richly rewarding inside. Effectively the family chapel of the Knightleys, it is crammed with their memorials and boasts a large squire's pew. There is also a fine collection of 16th-century Flemish stained glass.

A waymarked path between the lakes crosses one of the great 'laundes' or sheep pastures **D**. This gives a good feel of the 16th-century landscape, with sheep grazing amid the long views back over the hall, the church and the park.

FACT FILE

☀ Charwelton, 5 miles (8km) south-west of Daventry, on the A361

🗺 Pathfinder 999 (SP 45/55), grid reference SP 538561

miles 0	1	2	3	4	5	6	7	8	9	10 miles
kms 0	1 2	3	4 5	6	7 8	9	10 11	12	13 14 15	kms

◔ Allow 3 hours

▭ Mostly on good field paths. No steep inclines

P In the village or at the start

🍴 The Fox & Hounds in Charwelton

THE WALK

CHARWELTON – FAWSLEY

The walk starts at a large area suitable for parking, south-east of the A361 on the road to Canons Ashby.

1 Walk back to the crossroads with the A361. Take the bridleway signposted to Fawsley, by the roadsign to Canons Ashby. The path crosses the field diagonally to a stile beside a gate. Climb this and head well to the right of modern farm buildings to a stile. Cross this, ignoring the waymark disc pointing left, and continue ahead to the stile at the edge of the field. Climb this, cross the stream bed and go over the next gate. Turn

Fawsley Farm **A**, turn left to a road.

2 Turn right and descend past Fawsley Hall **B**. At a bend, turn right through the kissing-gate onto the waymarked Knightley Way. Beyond the church **C**, go between the two lakes and over a stile. Head slightly left, uphill through a field **D**, and follow a white waymark on a tree stump to reach the valley floor.

3 Turn right off the Knightley Way. Walk beside the hedge, going through a gate. Where the hedge turns left, go half-left across the field. The path should be clear; if not, keep walking parallel to the electricity lines.

4 Follow a farm track to a road. Turn right. The road climbs gradually. At a shallow right bend, where there are two black metal gates, look for a stile partly shaded by an oak tree on your left. Go over and follow the path towards a tall ash tree standing at the corner of a hedge.

5 Climb a stile left of the tree through the hedge. Go straight on through two fields, with the hedge on your right. At the end, follow the boundary round to a gate into the farmyard. Go past a stone barn on your right and through a gate. Cross the remains of Charwelton medieval village **E** to Holy Trinity Church **F**.

6 Go through the churchyard and out by a gate beyond the church tower. Cross the pasture, with the 'fish ponds' **G** on your left, to a stile. Continue ahead, parallel to the wooded valley floor, to a gate onto a road. Bear left into Charwelton **H**. At the main road, turn right.

7 Beyond the packhorse bridge **J**, cross to the bridleway on your left. Go through a gate and over pasture, with Charwelton Hall **K** to your left. Descend to the left of the old railway bridge. Go through a gate and turn right onto the road, which crosses the railway bridge and heads back to the crossroads near the start.

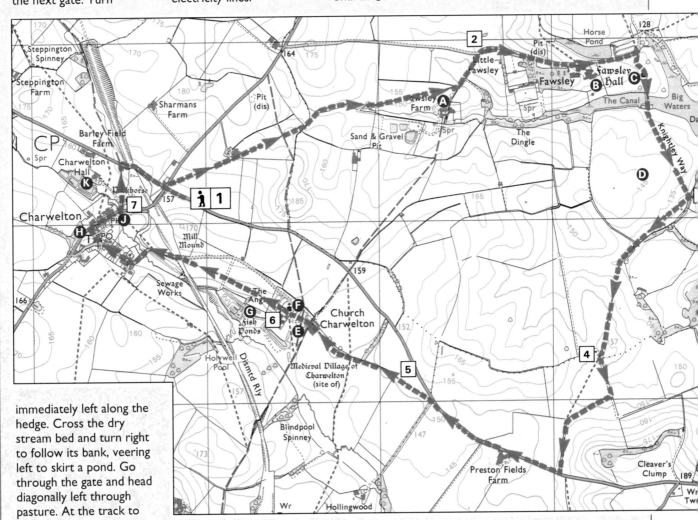

immediately left along the hedge. Cross the dry stream bed and turn right to follow its bank, veering left to skirt a pond. Go through the gate and head diagonally left through pasture. At the track to

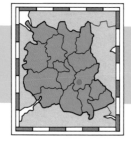
NORTHAMPTONSHIRE

MIKE WILLIAMS. INSET: M.J.GARWOOD/NHPA

Chapel. Members of the family have been buried in Great Brington since the 16th century. The 8th Earl Spencer, father of Princess Diana, joined his ancestors here in 1992.

There is a very fine collection of monuments in the chapel, which is closed off by its original Tudor railings. Between the chancel and the chapel are three canopied Tudor tombs, complete with effigies; many more cluster beyond. The oddest is that to Sir Edward Spencer (d.1655), set off in a corner, where he appears to be climbing out of his urn!

FOX COVERT

From the church, the route sets out past the Old Rectory of 1822, whose curious polygonal Scottish Baronial tower is a blunt counterpoint to that of the church.

You go through Chinkwell Spinney, a fox covert, to join a road alongside Althorp Park **B**. The park

◀ *As you walk through the woodland to the south-west of Lower Harlestone, you pass this charming, brick-built farmhouse. Fairies' bonnets (inset) grow on tree stumps in the woods.*

Lovely stone villages and mellow countryside around a stately home

Althorp, the family home of the Spencers for more than four centuries, is set in parkland amid delightful countryside and is ringed by several handsome villages. Many of the villages are largely built in mellow, golden Hornton limestone, which is known locally as Northamptonshire ironstone.

One of the best ironstone buildings is at the starting point of the walk. St Mary's Church **A**, superbly located at the north end of Great Brington, has a dominating battlemented west tower.

The interior is a spiky sea of poppyhead bench ends. The set was made up in 1846, using many medieval examples and some 57 carved in 1606. Near the south door is a rare survival, a Jacobean almsbox on a timber column.

The main reason for visiting the church, though, is the Spencer

---

FACT FILE

✳ Great Brington, 6 miles (9.6km) north-west of Northampton, off the A428

▱ Pathfinder 978 (SP 66/76), grid reference SP 667652

miles 0 1 2 3 4 5 6 7 8 9 10 miles
kms 0 1 2 3 4 5 6 7 8 9 10 11 12 13 14 15 kms

◐ Allow 3½ hours

▬ Easy going on lanes and clearly marked paths

P On roads in the village; please park considerately

🍴 The Fox & Hounds in Lower Harlestone, the Fox & Hounds in Great Brington, and Ye Olde Saracen's Head in Little Brington

I For details of the opening times of Althorp, and other tourist information, Tel. (01604) 22677

THE WALK

GREAT BRINGTON – HARLESTON – NOBOTTLE

The walk starts from Great Brington's church **A**.

1 Turn left to wind through the village. At the bend beyond the Fox and Hounds pub, turn left onto a lane, then left again just before The Stables. The clear track descends by a hedge, through the fields. Follow the path through a spinney, and over a stile onto a road. Turn right. Walk beside the wall of Althorp Park **B** to a junction. Turn left. Follow the road into Harlestone.

2 Beyond the thatched Park Cottage, go through a gate on your left, into a paddock. Head diagonally right uphill, then descend to the corner of the field to join a tarmac path. Go through a gate. Follow the path through another gate. Cross a small green in front of the village hall. Go through two more gates. Cross a golf course fairway and head for Harlestone's church. The ruined stables **C** are on your right.

3 At the church **D**, the path descends between stone walls. Continue across the junction on the raised causeway to the left. Go left, through a gate, and across pasture to another gate. Beyond this, bear right and go through a gate into a farmyard. At the road, turn right. Walk through Lower Harlestone.

4 Just before the Fox and Hounds, turn right at No. 34 in a terrace of thatched cottages. Just before a cattle grid, go through a gate and follow the path parallel to the stone wall. Bear left between two blocks of woodland. Follow the path to the right of a lodge. This leads straight ahead to a road. Turn right, and right again at the junction, downhill. Just before the valley bottom, turn left through a gate and follow the tarmac path through another gate to the road. Turn right, then left at a small green with a single horse chestnut tree. Almost immediately, turn right through a gate into a pasture. Go ahead and through a gate into a field. The path bears left to the far corner of Yewtree Spinney, then crosses a field diagonally. Make for a byre with a pantiled roof. Continue across the next field, then bear left to the corner of a wood. Walk with the main wood on your right. Keep ahead through a spur of the wood, then continue as before. At the next gate, bear half-left to a road in Nobottle **E**. Turn right.

5 Halfway down the hill, bear half-right over a stile, through pasture to a gate. Go through and continue ahead to a lane. Turn right. Go left through a gate at the next bend, then left through another gate. Walk across the field to a gate in the opposite hedge, and go half-right across the next field. Cross a stile and turn left along the green lane, into Little Brington **F**.

6 Just beyond Ye Olde Saracen's Head, go right on a gravel drive. The path continues between hedges. A stile at the end leads across pasture to another stile. Bear diagonally right (ignoring a path straight on). Cross a footbridge with a stile at each end and continue across the ridge-and-furrow **G**, towards a footpath. Turn left along the road, then left over a stile. Follow the hedge, then diverge to a stile in the far corner. Cross, and head for the corner diagonally opposite. Cross into a lane. Turn left, then right at the T-junction to head back to the start.

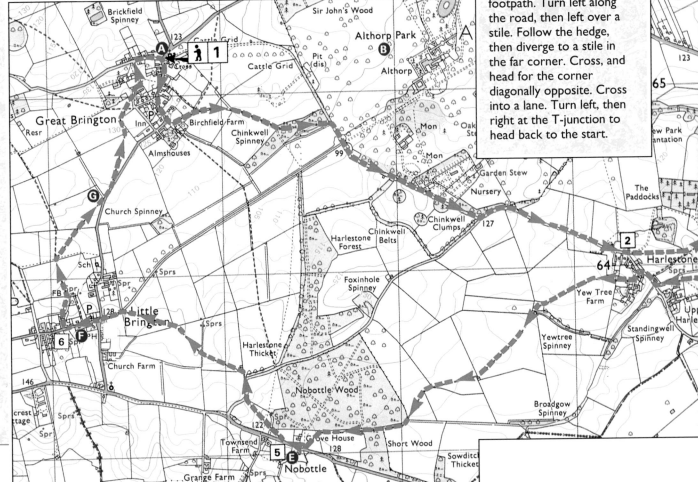

▲*In Great Brington's church, splendid tombs such as this one are monuments to the wealth of the Spencer family. On a house in Lower Harlestone is this interesting double sundial (below).*

was created in about 1512, when over 300 acres (120 hectares) were set aside behind a fence for the pursuit of pleasure and game alike. It looks much the same today, though a dry-stone wall has long replaced the fence, and most of the great trees are of a later date.

In the midst of the park is Althorp House, which can be seen from the road. The original Tudor mansion, much enlarged and altered, was clad in white brick, made from Cambridgeshire gault clay, in the late 18th century. At the same time, the moat was filled in and the formal gardens swept away.

PALLADIAN STABLES

The anaemic white brick is visually disappointing, but the Palladian stable block, in fiery local ironstone, is an altogether different matter. This well composed building can also be seen from the road.

The route next takes you into Harlestone, an interesting ironstone village that is scattered along a small, steep, winding valley. The Northampton Golf Clubhouse, a two-storey modern building, looks over an artificial lake whose dam masquerades as a rusticated three-arched bridge. The clubhouse occupies the site of Harlestone House, demolished in 1940. The old mansion was one of many claimed to be the model for Jane Austen's *Mansfield Park*.

The old house's Palladian stables **C** remain, a ruin of spectacular and monumental beauty. They are similar to those at Althorp, in that they have corner pavilions and central, arched portico throughways,

▶*This cylindrical dovecote in Harlestone is topped by leaded glass.*

▲*Lychgates, such as this one at St Andrew's, Harlestone, provided shade in which to rest a body prior to burial.*

but they are sadly dilapidated.

St Andrew's Church **D**, just beyond the stable block, is well documented in the manorial estate book of Henry de Bray, a rich source of local history. The chancel was built around 1320 and the nave by 1325, but the tower must be earlier; a bell-rope was bought in 1294. Inside, there are many interesting things to see, including a two-bay crypt, a good font, a pulpit dating from around 1500 with Flemish panels,

whose spire is visible from miles around. There are many Spencer estate cottages here, as well as good ironstone buildings.

The route back to Great Brington crosses some of the most spectacular ridge-and-furrow land **G** in a county where many thousands of acres of these relics of medieval, communally farmed ploughland survive in the pastures.

Many communal fields were swept away by graziers, such as the Spencers, who destroyed villages and enclosed the land for sheep runs in the 15th and 16th centuries. Others fell victim to enclosure by Act of Parliament, particularly in the 18th century. Here, the furrows are so deep and the ridges so high that walking across them is like a ride on a roller-coaster.

▲ *Just before the route reaches Nobottle Wood, the scene is one of rural tranquillity. At the end of the walk (left), there is a fine view across the countryside from St Mary's Church.*

and a very handsome west gallery.

You continue through Lower Harlestone, passing the Georgian old rectory (now called Harlestone House) and a school by George Devey, a Victorian architect who specialized in domestic styles. The pastures within the village contain many signs of former houses and closes; the village was originally more densely built up.

VICTORIAN TUDOR

Here, and in the other villages on the walk, are occasional Spencer estate cottages of the 1840s and 1850s. They are built in picturesque Tudor style, with leaded lattice casements in timber-mullioned window frames, and steep gables.

Across the fields, past the ancient Nobottle Wood on the parish boundary, is Nobottle **E**, a medieval village now reduced to a few farms and cottages. The heart of the village was in the fields immediately west of the aptly named Townsend Farm.

You approach the village of Little Brington **F** on an oak-lined avenue, the end of a carriage road that ran for 2 miles (3.2km) from Althorp and is now a disused green lane. The village has a Victorian church,

The Spencer Dynasty

John Spencer, a grazier, bought the Althorp estate in 1508, and soon turned much of it into a park. He lived at Wormleighton in Warwickshire, and used Althorp's manor house as a hunting lodge.

Wealth derived from wool production enabled the Spencers to rise through the ranks of the local gentry, assisted by judicious marriages to heiresses. They enclosed and destroyed villages to provide enormous sheep runs at both Wormleighton and Althorp, supporting nearly 20,000 animals.

The Spencer tombs in Great Brington church record their social progress. John Spencer was knighted, although his farming activities were scrutinized by Wolsey's Enclosure Commissioners in 1517. His son rebuilt the manor house, and

Robert, his great-great-grandson, was created Baron Spencer in 1603.

The family moved to Althorp in the 17th century. The Tudor house was enlarged and remodelled to frame a gated court with bridges across the moat, formal terraces and parterres. Fashionable pilasters and cornices concealed the Tudor core.

The title of Earl Spencer was created in 1765; the current Earl, Princess Diana's brother, is the 9th. In 1787-91, the 2nd Earl employed Henry Holland to give the house its present appearance. He also had the park landscaped. The Spencers were prominent in politics and the Victorian earls stamped their identity on the estate villages, building many cottages and almshouses.

The 1st Earl Spencer and his wife.

15

COTSWOLD GARDENS

A walk via Cotswold villages to beautiful gardens

This walk through a designated Area of Outstanding Natural Beauty takes in several typical Cotswold villages. Here there are lovely cottages of butter-hued limestone — often capped with dipping thatch or traditional stone slates diminishing in size towards the top pitch. In summer, roses seem to cling to the houses and many old-fashioned, perennial flowers bloom in the gardens.

The route climbs to about 600 feet (183 metres) and gives wide views over the Avon vale towards the rounded Bredon Hill and the Malvern hills in the distance.

The lovely village of Mickleton **A** — with its thatched, timber-framed

FACT FILE

- Mickleton, North Gloucestershire, 3 miles (5 km) north of Chipping Campden

- Pathfinder 1020 (SP 04/14), grid reference SP 16435

miles 0 1 2 3 4 5 6 7 8 9 10 miles
kms 0 1 2 3 4 5 6 7 8 9 10 11 12 13 14 15 kms

- Allow 2¼ hours

- Easy paths over fields and through woods. Steep in places. Stout shoes recommended

- **P** Cul-de-sac lane off B4632, Mickleton (opposite Lloyds Bank)

- Pubs and hotel at Mickleton. Restaurant and shop at Hidcote Manor Garden

- Hidcote Manor Garden: Open April to end October. Check opening times. Admission charge

- Kiftsgate Court Gardens: Open April to end September. Check opening times. Admission charge

▲ *The spectacular gardens of Hidcote Manor in the hamlet of Hidcote Bartrim. (inset) Red foxes are numerous but elusive animals in the Cotswolds.*
◀ *A quiet corner in the charming garden at Kiftsgate Court.*

cottages — is centred around a Victorian memorial fountain. And nearby, the church of St Lawrence dates from Saxon times, although the spire was added in 1352.

WOODS AND HAMLETS

The woods of Bakers Hill **B** are mixed coppice and beech. In the past coppiced trees were cut periodically quite near the ground to provide branches for sheep hurdles. These upland beechwoods are very colourful in the autumn. Hidcote Boyce **C** is a hamlet of a few cottages, many built at right angles to the road so the frontage was small and the garden long in the days when these were the homes of farmers and their families.

THE ELIZABETHAN MANOR

Hidcote Manor **E** has one of the most delightful gardens in England. It was the home of the great horticulturist Major Lawrence Johnston. He spent almost 40 years converting ten acres of grassland on a high inhospitable site into magnificent gardens, now renowned for their

THE WALK

MICKLETON – HIDCOTE

The walk begins from a cul-de-sac off the B4632 in Mickleton Ⓐ, opposite Lloyds Bank.

1 Walk along the cul-de-sac lane past the church to a footpath signpost. The way is up the bank, right. Go through a kissing gate to enter a pasture. Keep to the right and go through a gate to the woods.

2 Walk along a twisting path leading to a hill pasture. Go through a gate and, keeping to left-hand side, walk up through a field to go through a gap. Bear right uphill and follow alongside a wood on the left to a lane.

3 Cross to the signposted path opposite. Continue up through the short wood then along the side of a field (the wood is on the right).

4 Go through a gateway (the gate is missing) and enter the woods at Baker's Hill Ⓑ. Follow the well-worn track out of the woods to a barn and tarmac farm way. Turn left, then immediately right to walk by

the border of a field alongside a hedge on the left.

5 Cross a brook by a plank bridge and enter the next field. Turn left and walk around two corners of a field to reach a broken field gate (there is a faint waymark sign on a post).

6 Turn left and walk along a grassy track to a road. Cross to the lane to Hidcote Boyce Ⓒ. As the lane twists right walk straight on by a stone water trough to Top Farm.

7 Walk past the house and barn and go through a kissing gate. Bear left over the field and walk to a high step-stile and footbridge across a brook. Keep on this heading passing an isolated tree to the farm Ⓓ at Hidcote Bartrim. Go through two five-bar gates and follow the lane to Hidcote Manor Garden Ⓔ. Stop here to visit the gardens.

8 Walk along the lane which turns left by the car park entrance to a junction of ways by Kiftsgate Court Ⓕ. Stop to visit gardens.

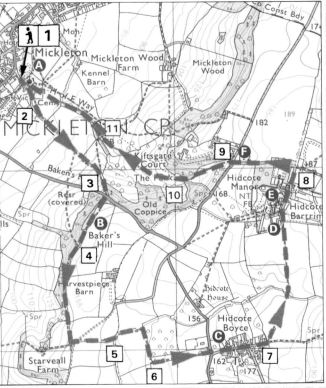

9 Cross the road and go through a gate into a hill pasture. Walk down the length of the field and pass into the next field by waymarked post.

10 Walk along the bridleway, marked by a blue arrow, keeping to the left-hand side of pasture, next to woods, to a small gate.

11 Proceed along field edge with trees on left and Mickleton Church spire coming into view. Walk through last gateway and cross field to church and starting point.

▲ *The pretty hamlet of Hidcote Boyce in the heart of the Cotswolds.*
▶ *The flower-decked water fountain in the middle of Mickleton village.*

rare shrubs, trees and herbaceous borders. Hidcote was given to the National Trust in 1948.

About ¼ mile (400 metres) along a lane from Hidcote is another garden open to the public. The hillside garden of Kiftsgate Court Ⓕ was built at the end of the last century. The gardens contain many fine specimens of colourful and unusual trees and shrubs. Plants are often on sale to the public.

FARMING AND WILDLIFE

The alkaline soil of the Cotswolds has always provided ideal grassland for sheep farming — an important source of wealth since Roman times. During the last war it was discovered that the land could also produce good arable crops.

Common flowers found in the area include cowslips, orchids, thyme, primroses, rock roses and vetches. At springtime bluebells are prolific in lower woodlands and butterflies love the meadow grasses. And constantly heard but rarely seen are the skylarks.

THE WOOL TRAIL

16

GLOUCESTERSHIRE

FACT FILE

☀ Tiltups End, on the A46, 2 miles (3 km) south of Nailsworth

▱ Pathfinder 1133 (ST 89/99), grid reference ST 845971

miles 0 1 2 3 4 5 6 7 8 9 10 miles
kms 0 1 2 3 4 5 6 7 8 9 10 11 12 13 14 15 kms

◔ Allow 4-5 hours

▭ Mostly easy walking. Walking boots recommended. Not suitable for children

P Large pub car park plus parking on cut-off section of old road at Tiltups End; parking in Nailsworth is difficult

▦ Tipputs Inn. The Cross Inn and two shops in Avening; a range of facilities in Nailsworth; Bell & Castle pub at Horsley

Through Cotswold villages once at the heart of the wool trade

BELOW LEFT & RIGHT: PAUL FELIX. INSET E. A. JANES/NHPA

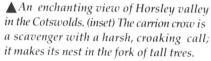

The walk begins with a long, slow descent from the top of the Cotswold plateau **A** to the old wool village of Avening. This is a fairly open landscape, in striking contrast to the later stages of the walk, where there are deep valleys, villages, old mills and ponds. Much of the initial route follows Ledgemore Bottom, a classic dry valley. Rainwater sinks rapidly

▲ *From a ridge beyond the village of Avening there is a fine view of Gatcombe Park, the home of The Princess Royal and her family.*
◀ *The Church of the Holy Cross in Avening was founded in 1070 and has an impressive tower at its centre.*

▲ *An enchanting view of Horsley valley in the Cotswolds. (inset) The carrion crow is a scavenger with a harsh, croaking call; it makes its nest in the fork of tall trees.*

down through the limestone rock of the Cotswolds, and the valley bottom only contains running streams immediately after heavy rain, although damp patches can be found here and there. These plateaulands were traditionally pasture for sheep, whose wool brought wealth to the region. The area is notable for wild-flowers such as toadflax.

HOME INDUSTRIES

Avening itself is a long-established settlement, as shown by the numerous prehistoric remains nearby; the best long barrows are north of the village, notably the Tingle Stone. The village was a centre of the early woollen industry, when weavers worked at home, and there are few industrial remains; a few old clothiers' houses, on three floors with large upstairs workshops, can be

51

THE WALK

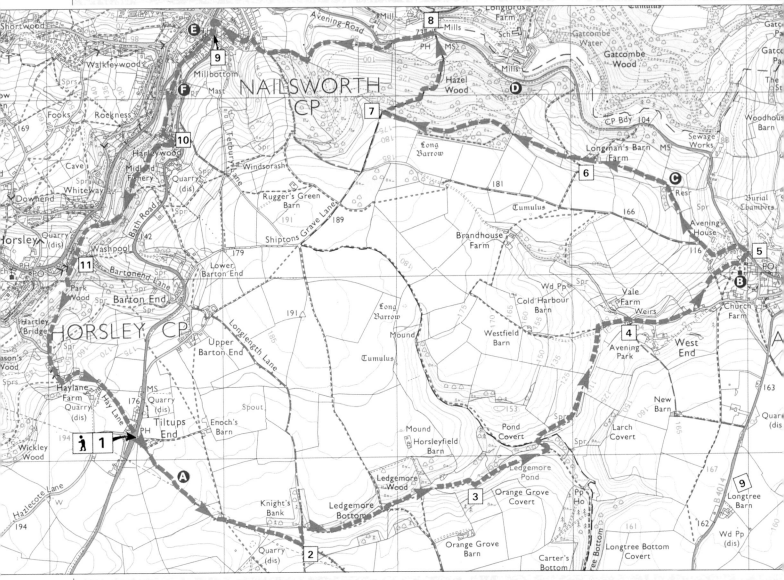

AVENING - NAILSWORTH

The walk begins at Tipputs Inn, Tiltups End, on the A46 south of Nailsworth. (An alternative starting point is Nailsworth Town Hall. Follow instructions from 9.)

▶ Cross main road to start of track, to right of sign marking 'The Old Rick Yard'. When track forks after 30 yards (27 metres) keep straight on and continue down to right-hand side of field Ⓐ, passing through two gates, then in the third field keeping close to fence and wood on left. Continue on track through two more gates uphill to reach concrete farm road.

▶2 Turn left through metal gate and follow road downhill for 80 yards (70 metres), then turn right down valley keeping wood on left. At end of field, go through gate in middle of wall ahead and continue down valley, ignoring cross track. Go over stile to right of metal gate, and continue ahead, keeping just to left of valley bottom. When fence comes in from right, maintain direction alongside fence, but when fence ends turn right to cross stream, then go through gate into another field.

▶3 Turn left down valley, staying close to fence/wall and wood on left. When the wall ends, follow it round to the left and through gate. Turn right towards field gate at projecting corner of field, then continue forward with fence on right. At next corner, go over stile into small enclosure containing young trees; maintain direction alongside fence and leave enclosure by another stile. At bottom right corner of field, go through gate into enclosure and then cross stream by small stone footbridge beside ford, continuing over stile on to track between stone walls to reach road.

▶4 Turn right along road for 350 yards (290 metres) and after passing drive to 'Heron's Mead' turn left over stile just before next house's garage. Descend down side of garden; at end go right over stone stile into paddock. Keeping close to fence on right, go over stile into second paddock, drop down half left to stile to right of bottom corner.

Maintain direction to stile at far left corner of paddock. Ignore path to left crossing stream, and continue straight ahead over stile into another enclosure, with fence on left. At far corner, go over stile then slightly uphill towards stile at far right corner, which leads on to a path between stone walls.

To visit Avening church **B**, go immediately right into churchyard; otherwise continue down path to road, then right beside stream to reach main road in middle of village. Avening Post Office is uphill on left; the Cross Inn is 400 yards (360 metres) further up the main road.

5 To continue walk, turn left along main road towards Nailsworth, but immediately after petrol station turn left down Woodstock Lane. When track forks, keep right on unsurfaced track, with high wall to right. Climb for 100 yards (90 metres) and again fork right, with the track now levelling out. When vehicle track bears left to enter barnyard, keep right and continue on slightly overgrown green lane (with a fine view **C** of Gatcombe Park) until it emerges into field. Maintain direction across field, going slightly uphill, and when Longman's Barn becomes visible ahead make for metal gate in line with farm buildings.

6 Remain on track to left of farm buildings. Join better quality track emerging from farm; when this bends sharp right and uphill, continue forward through gate. Continue on rough track gently uphill across field to enter wood. At junction of paths just inside wood, take path ahead signed as bridleway. Follow yellow waymarks through wood until way ahead is blocked and there are bridleways signed to both left and right.

7 Turn right and downhill on sunken way; ignore crossing tracks until you reach junction of paths at bottom edge of wood. Go over stile into field and continue downhill, keeping just to left of line of trees. At the bottom of the field it is necessary to drop into the old sunken way, which sometimes doubles as a stream bed, to reach road by gate/stile. Turn left along road; the Weighbridge public house is immediately on the left (near Longford's Mill **D**).

8 Continue along road for 200 yards (180 metres) then bear left on a track going slightly uphill, marked by a footpath sign on the opposite side of the road. Enter field by gate/stile, and continue ahead on level track, passing farm buildings and staying close to right-hand edge of field. Path descends into wood and turns left into minor valley. Go over stile, then over a small stream and continue around to right just inside edge of wood. At far right corner of wood enter field with fence on right. Meet bridleway coming downhill from left, and turn right through gate.

A few yards after gate, go left up bank on clear path, leading to squeeze-stile and path descending steeply between hedges. At bottom, turn left along residential road and follow this to main A46. Turn left on A46 then almost immediately right into Old Bristol Road, to reach Nailsworth Town Hall **E** . (The alternative start.)

9 Turn right down steep pathway with County Council sign a few yards after Town Hall, then go left at bottom along alley with railings. This eventually leads back into Old Bristol Road. After 20 yards (18 metres) bear left on a footpath rising away from road. After 30 yards (27 metres) fork right on path parallel with road, dropping down to emerge at a small group of houses with Ruskin Mill **F** on the right. Continue ahead and uphill on path between houses and a mill, until you emerge beside a millpond. Continue alongside pond, then at end, ascend towards a group of houses. At top, turn left up short flight of steps then right along narrow access road which bends round to left and then to right.

10 After passing a house called 'Prencott' on the right when the road bends sharply left, continue forward on narrow path between two garages, then over stile into field. Keep close to fence on right and over stile in next field. Follow path bearing slightly away from fence on right. This rises slightly then runs across open slope to enter wood by stone stile. In wood go straight ahead and downhill, then go over stile by garage. Continue forward on path to left of a house called 'Leylandia'. Cross stream then turn left to access road following stream. Road narrows to footpath and passes a pair of cottages on right to reach another road. For Horsley village turn right and go up hill.

11 Unless visiting Horsley, go directly ahead on track running up right-hand side of clearing. After 100 yards (90 metres) at fork at end of clearing, take left-hand minor path uphill, which soon joins another path coming in from right. Ascend steadily on fairly well-defined footpath going diagonally up through wood to reach stile into field; this section might be difficult to follow in winter. Maintain direction up field to pylon, then continue downhill to gate/stile. Turn left and uphill on minor road for 1/3 mile (500 metres) to reach A46.

found near the church in Avening.

The Church of the Holy Cross **B** once belonged to the Abbess of the Holy Trinity, at Caen in France.

THE NORMAN CHURCH

Dating from the early Norman period, the church is shaped like a cross with the tower at the centre. The interior includes a monument to Henry Bridges, son of Lord Chandos of Sudeley, and a notorious pirate; he

PAUL FELIX

Nailsworth, a town of steep, narrow streets, has many fine Georgian and Jacobean merchants' houses, dating from the time when it was a major wool centre. The weavers' cottages can still be seen along the roadside.

lived at Avening Court, just to the east of the village and died in 1615. The most attractive parts of Avening are by the stream, between the church and the Post Office.

Beyond Avening, the walk climbs back on to the ridge, and there is a fine view **C** across the valley to

Gatcombe Park, once the residence of the 19th-century economist David Ricardo, and currently of the Princess Royal.

MILL VALLEYS

Dropping down again into the valley, the walk passes near Longford's Mill **D**, just east of the Weighbridge Inn. This mill continued in production until 1990, remaining profitable because it had the largest mill pond in the area and hence the most reliable power. The pond cost £1000 to build in the early l9th century and covered a total of 15 acres (6 hectares).

The path then approaches the mill town of Nailsworth through the woods, but avoids the town centre, which contains few old buildings; the parish church dates from only 1898. There is a good view over some of the older parts of the town from near the Town Hall **E**.

THE TOP OF THE PLATEAU

The walk then follows paths and alleys up a side valley towards Horsley, which contains several old mills and two large millponds. Ruskin Mill **F** still has a millwheel, and the large pond behind is home to ducks and moorhens. There was

The 19th-century church of St Martin's is one of many churches built on the same site in Horsley, yet its fine tower has been there since Norman times.

a corn mill on roughly this site as early as 1564. From here the path climbs to the little weaving hamlet of Harleywood, then through the woods above the Midland Fisheries – another large mill pond more recently used for fish farming – back up to the top of the plateau. On the way there is a fine view back to St Martin's Church in Horsley, with its impressive Norman tower.

There are several attractive old mills with mill ponds in the village of Horsley, including Ruskin Mill where there was once a 16th-century corn mill.

The Cotswold Wool Industry

Until the decline of the wool trade, fleece was an important commodity and many manors and churches in the Cotswolds towns and villages were built with its profits.

Since the 19th century, the centre of the British wool industry has been the West Riding of Yorkshire. However, before the Industrial Revolution there were two main centres – East Anglia (Norfolk and Suffolk), which made lightweight worsted cloth, and the West Country, making heavier woollen cloth and centred around Trowbridge in Wiltshire and Stroud in Gloucestershire.

Until the Industrial Revolution, weaving went on not in factories but in people's homes where whole families worked together using hand looms. In the Cotswolds, villages on the edge of the plateau were the main weaving centres. In 1608, there were 17 weavers listed in Avening, and 40 in Horsley.

In the early 19th century, the industry and the region were transformed. Two hundred new mills, or related buildings, were built with mill ponds behind them to provide a steady supply of water power, and new turnpike roads along the now drier valley bottoms connected the factories to their village markets.

The valley town of Nailsworth is almost entirely a creation of the 19th-century cloth industry, with at least 40 mills. However, despite this expansion, the Cotswolds lacked the abundant fast-flowing streams of the Pennines, and as the wool industry became increasingly factory-based and mechanised, the importance of the Cotswolds as a wool producer inevitably declined.

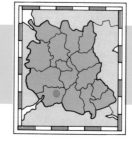
GLOUCESTERSHIRE

A scenic walk from a Saxon village along the Cotswold Way

This walk has something for all the family. The route goes to the top of the Cotswolds escarpment and offers magnificent views. There are archaeological sites, an historic castle, and beautiful formal and cottage gardens. In addition, you can visit a unique railway museum and if, towards the end of the walk, youngsters have the energy they can enjoy an exciting adventure playground – including a junior-sized rustic castle.

HISTORIC MEMORABILIA

The starting place is Winchcombe **A**, a small town built of whitish limestone beside the little River Isbourne. It dates from Saxon times when it was a walled city.

Kenulf ruled the kingdom of

FACT FILE

* Winchcombe, 6 miles (10 km) north-east of Cheltenham

* Pathfinder 1067 (SP02/12), grid reference, SP 022282

miles 0 1 2 3 4 5 6 7 8 9 10 miles
kms 0 1 2 3 4 5 6 7 8 9 10 11 12 13 14 15 kms

* Allow 3 hours

* Easy paths in fields and woods but quite steep and rocky in places

* **P** Back Lane, off North Street, behind the library

* Hotels, inns in Winchcombe. Restaurant, Sudeley Castle

* **WC** Winchcombe and in Sudeley Castle (by car park)

* Sudeley Castle and gardens open from Easter to October. Admission charge. Winchcombe railway museum and gardens are open at weekends and daily in August. Admission charge

▲ *The soils of Sudeley hill are mainly grainy limestone, encouraging a variety of flowers. This is ideal for butterflies, including the Duke of Burgundy Fritillary (inset). Winchcombe (below) contains many buildings of architectural interest.*

DEREK FORSS INSET: SWIFT PICTURE LIBRARY

DEREK FORSS

THE WALK

WINCHCOMBE

The walk starts from St Peter's Church, Winchcombe **A** *on the B4632 (formerly A46) road between Cheltenham and Stratford.*

1 Walk along the main street towards Cheltenham. Within 200 yards (180 metres) and opposite the railway museum **B** turn left along Mill Lane (the road drops downhill). By a bicycle sign turn right along a wide path bordered by a hedge and a wall. Cross the River Isbourne **C**. The path is signposted to divide.

2 Take the left fork to pass to the right of the sports pavilion and go into a pasture through a wooden kissing gate. Walk to the far diagonal corner of the field.

3 Climb a stone stile to a lane. Turn left and continue for ¼ mile (400 metres). Bear right through a gate and along the vehicle drive (signposted as a footpath to 'Belas Knap'). Past the cricket field the vehicle drive veers sharply to the right. Walk on and go over a step stile and climb the sheeplands, passing just to the right of an isolated oak tree. Go to a step stile in the far top of the field. Continue over a meadow to a stone step stile on to a lane.

4 Turn right (Corndean Lane). The lane climbs gently and, when it divides, take the left-hand fork. Still climbing, go past Corndean woodlands **D** and some farm buildings at Hill Barn Farm. Follow a rough and stony farm road.

5 Within 400 yards (360 metres) at a junction of farm tracks, turn left. The path, signposted 'Belas Knap and Cotswold Way' is at the edge of a field alongside a traditional Cotswold stone wall. Climb a wall stile to Belas

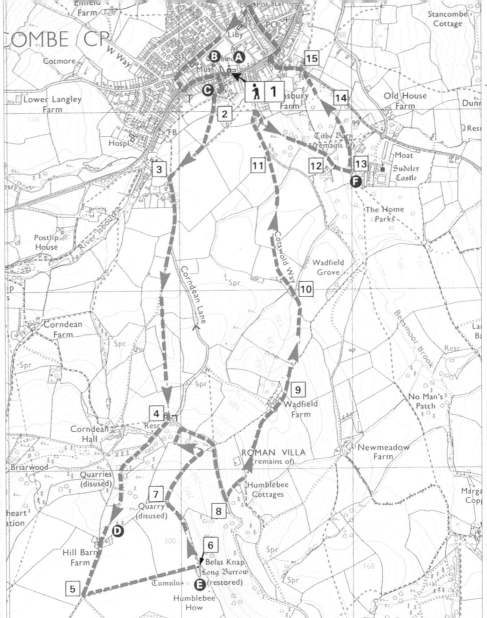

Knap Long Barrow **E**.

6 Leave the Barrow and go over a wall and through a metal kissing gate. The path goes left then right and runs alongside the edge of a field (woods on right) and a stone wall. Go through another kissing gate.

7 Walk between the two sides of a sheep pasture to a third metal kissing gate leading to a clear, well-used track to a road. Turn right for 700 yards (630 metres) towards privately owned Humblebee Cottages.

8 Turn to the left, signposted 'Cotswold Way' and pass by the cottages. Follow the farm vehicle way that bears left. Continue to the right of some barns and the

privately owned Wadfield House.

9 Walk along a fenced way to a field. Go over a step stile. Stay by a right-hand hedge, walking down to climb a step stile.

10 Turn left and walk by a left-hand hedge. A short distance around the bottom corner of the field go over a plank bridge and stile. Continue diagonally over the next field towards a marker post and stay on this course. Stiles and arrows show the way to a road.

11 Turn left and continue for 400 yards (360 metres) to the entrance, by a farm, to the grounds of Sudeley Castle **F**. Turn right along the drive (the public footpath

is signposted). Go over a bridge to the next cattle grid.

12 Go right, through a metal gate. Keep alongside the adventure playground (on left) to pass through a kissing gate.

13 Bear left, walking by the left-hand fence (paybox for admission to the Castle is by the car park, right). Cross a drive using the step stiles into a field.

14 Walk over the field and go through a kissing gate leading to a large sheep pasture. Walk towards the far corner.

15 Go through a gate to a lane. Turn left and follow the route shown on the map through town.

PAUL FELIX

◀ *This grotesque gargoyle was carved in the 15th century on Winchcombe Church.*

full of interesting features inside and incorporates some stones from the Abbey. But the most startling exterior item is the array of ugly gargoyles. There are 40 in all and they may have been carved by townsfolk to represent unpopular members of the monastic order.

Seen from the outside, no. 22, Gloucester Street, in Winchcombe **B** looks like an ordinary terraced house. However, down the narrow passageway alongside is a wonderland of memorabilia of a past age. This is a museum of railway life — 'things to do, things to see and things to remember'. For the gardener, there is an area laid out with old and rare plants — a Victorian vegetable garden and herbs.

MEDIEVAL MAGIC

The powerful little River Isbourne **C** that cuts through the town from the high wolds, once powered many mills, including paper mills. There are reminders today, including Mill Lane and Silk Mill Lane. Duck Street

Mercia from 796 and founded a great Benedictine abbey at Winchcombe. This was to become a seat of learning and the arts and attracted prelates and pilgrims. Little remains of the buildings today but near the site is the magnificent 15th-century St Peter's Church. It is

▼ *Belas Knap – a fine example of a Bronze Age burial mound built 4,000 years ago.*

PAUL FELIX

Nature Walk

THE KESTREL, hovering in flight and watching for its prey of small mammals and birds, is a familiar sight in the Cotswolds.

CHRIS ROSE

When the kestrel is in flight, its wings are pointed and the long tail is held closed. When the bird is hovering the tail is fanned out to give stability. Kestrels hover, adjusting their tail angle according to wind speed.

The kestrel is well-adapted for its hunting lifestyle. Talons are sharp for seizing prey and its bill is hooked to tear flesh.

S & O MATHEWS

◄ Sheep farming is widespread in the Cotswolds. Local limestone is used for building the characteristic drystone walls.

(18 metres) wide and 18 feet (5 metres) high, with four burial chambers. When first excavated in 1863-5, 38 skeletons were discovered together with implements and pottery. The original drystone walls of the barrow are interesting as they confirm that the waller's art has survived for at least 4,000 years.

WOODS AND PARKLAND

Near Belas Knap the walk joins the Cotswold Way — the long-distance waymarked footpath which runs for over 100 miles (160 km) from Chipping Campden to Bath, following existing rights-of-way. The path by Humblebee Cottages goes below a little wood.

Nearing Winchcombe again, signposted pathways lead through parkland to the grand, partly ruined castle of Sudeley **F**. Collections of toys, antiques and armour make the castle well worth a visit.

(now Vineyard Street) indicates where the ducking stool to punish witches was sited. The public stocks are still displayed in the town and were in use, for the humiliation of drunkards, as late as 1860.

The route climbs past Corndean woodlands **D** to Belas Knap **E**. The latter is said to be one of the finest specimens of neolithic long barrows in the country. Built about 2000 BC, it is 178 feet (55 metres) long, 60 feet

Sudeley Castle

The privately owned castle near Winchcombe has royal connections that started as far back as the 9th century, when the estate was owned by Ethelred the Unready.

In the middle of the 14th century the castle came into the hands of the Boteler family. Ralph Boteler was granted the title of Baron Sudeley and rebuilt the fortification in the mid-15th century with the spoils of Henry V's wars. During the Wars of the Roses the baron backed the wrong side and the castle reverted to Edward IV.

Catherine of Aragon stayed at the castle and Anne Boleyn came with Henry VIII. Thomas Seymour (who became Lord Sudeley) married Henry's widow, Katherine Parr. She lies buried in the castle's chapel of St Mary.

Sudeley Castle was partly destroyed at the end of the Civil War and from the middle of the 17th to the beginning of the 19th century it lay a neglected ruin. Parts were made habitable again in 1840. Today, it is a collection of splendid buildings and roofless ruins (including the Elizabethan banqueting hall and the barn).

In the house there are art treasures and paintings by Turner, Rubens and Van Dyck. In addition, there are magnificent gardens (including the formally patterned flower garden or 'parterre', planted with old-fashioned roses in herb-edged beds). Sudeley Castle is

also home to a working community of craftsmen, and offers an adventure playground and falconry courses.

Sudley Castle is rich in Tudor history. Its extensive gardens are a further attraction and there is also a specialist garden centre.

BTA/ETB/SI

REDMARLEY

Dick Whittington's birthplace to a tiny gorge and vineyard

Stunning scenery is not the only feature of this walk in deepest Gloucestershire: there is history and legend too, for it is here that London's most famous Lord Mayor, Dick Whittington, was born. Another, more unexpected, local 'product' is the wine of the area, made from grapes grown on the slopes above the River Leadon.

RED ROCK

As you start the walk, you can see, to the south, May Hill and the uplands of the Forest of Dean. On your return to Redmarley, you will see ahead the most spectacular moorland ridge of the Malvern Hills, built on some of the most ancient rock in southern Britain.

The rock of the Redmarley area creates a gentler but still striking landscape. It gives the soil, and

▲During the Ice Age, ice and melt-water carved out lakes such as this one in the Leadon valley. A newly emerged comma butterfly (inset). Its bark-like wings provide ideal camouflage.

FACT FILE

⁎ Redmarley D'Abitot, 10 miles (16 km) north-west of Gloucester, just off A147 and south of Junction 2 on M50

os Pathfinders 1041(SO 63/73) and 1065 (SO 62/72), grid reference SO 752313

miles 0 1 2 3 4 5 6 7 8 9 10 miles
kms 0 1 2 3 4 5 6 7 8 9 10 11 12 13 14 15 kms

◖ Allow 3½-4 hours

▬ Easy walking, mainly on farm tracks with some woodland paths; may be very muddy after rain, so walking shoes are recommended

P Restricted roadside parking in Redmarley village

🍴 Rose and Crown pub and shops at Playley Green on A147, 1 mile (1.6 km) east of Redmarley

I Three Choirs Vineyard: free wine tasting, Tel. (01531) 890555

---

many of the buildings, a rich, red glow, from which Redmarley derives its name.

St Bartholomew's Church was rebuilt in the 19th century, but it contains many interesting features. In the village there are also several timber-framed buildings, which date from the 1500s.

From Redmarley you descend into the Leadon valley to Pauntley, walking parallel to the river. Pauntley Court was the home of the Whittington family between 1311 and 1546 and two of the church's windows carry their coat of arms. The present house, which is closed to the public, mainly dates from the 18th century, but a half-timbered wing, for long used as a granary,

THE WALK

REDMARLEY D'ABITOT – LEADON VALLEY

The walk begins at the entrance to Redmarley Church.

01 With the church behind you, turn right along the village street for 50 yards (46 metres), then left down the road just before Well House Cottage. After 60 yards (55 metres), turn left through gate, following bridleway sign, and then fork left. Follow track between fences until it emerges through a gate, then turn left. On reaching road at junction, continue ahead following sign to Newent. Drop steeply down on road, ignoring side turns, as it runs through a cutting in the sandstone between overhanging woods, to cross the Leadon at Playford Bridge.

2 After 100 yards (91 metres), just before first house, turn left and climb over gate into field. Keep close to hedge on right; when this swings round to right, Pauntley Court is visible ahead and the path becomes clearer. At the end of field, go forward through gate and ahead on a track which swings right and uphill to emerge in open area outside Pauntley Church **A**. Turn right and follow access road up to major road.

3 Cross the road and go through field gate just to the left. Continue forward, keeping hedge on right, through three fields, descending into a minor valley. At the corner of the third field, pass under electric fence to go right through gateway and immediately left, alongside

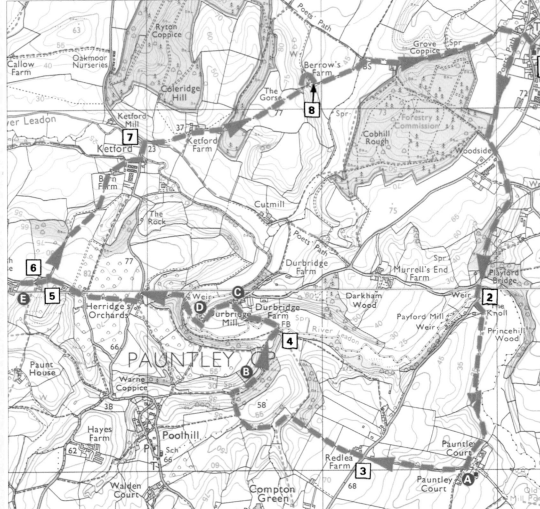

hedge, to reach another track. Go left through the gate and follow the track up the valley for 100 yards (91 metres), then right through a gate immediately to the left of the old hollow tree. Follow fence on the left, swinging sharply round to right over rise. At next corner, go forward over stile, then descend down left-hand edge of wood to meet another path at T-junction and turn right. At the end of first lake **B**, turn left over causeway, go through gate, then right. Go through another gate when level with end of second lake, then ahead over footbridge in line with end of third lake.

4 Turn left along bank, but when level with a sandstone outcrop on right continue forward and uphill on clear path. Go out through gate immediately to left of Durbridge Farm **C**. Turn left and descend on farm lane to Durbridge Mill **D**. Go through metal gate and keep to left of farm buildings; at end of buildings, swing round to right, then cross the bridge over the Leadon. Turn right along bank, but almost immediately fork left through gate at end of wood and follow track, just to right of row of trees. This climbs up to a road by the small cluster of farm

buildings. Turn left on road for 40 yards (37 metres), then right on concrete track between the vineyards. Meet a road at the corner and continue on it for 200 yards (183 metres); there is another vineyard on the left.

5 To reach the Three Choirs winery **E**, continue along the road for another 200 yards (183 metres), passing more vineyards on the left. From the winery, return along the road to Stage 6.

6 Turn left up a track between fences. Once over rise, the track narrows and passes large rabbit warren in bank on right. Keep on to bottom of hill, ignoring track on left half-way down. Enter field and cross half-right to gate at left-hand end of row of poplars. Follow public footpath or walk around the right-hand edge of the field towards farm. Enter yard by gate, then turn left to avoid farm buildings, cross parking area and follow farm track to road. Turn left to cross the Leadon.

7 At next bend, turn right over cattle grid and follow farm road up to Ketford Farm. Avoiding farmhouse, go through gate on right and walk through field, keeping close to hedge on right. Continue forward towards isolated oak tree, then over stile beyond. Turn left for 5 yards (4 metres), then diagonally uphill on path, initially indistinct, through young conifers. At top of hill, go over stile to left of corner of field then across large field: aim for left of middle of the largest gap between trees visible on skyline; when hill beyond appears, head for the radio mast. Leave by gate at far corner, then ahead and down hill on track, turning right at bottom.

8 Follow track past derelict Berrow's Farm into next field, then immediately turn left through gate and along left-hand side of field. When edge of field bends left, turn less sharply left across field to stile formed by metal railing. Cross this and follow right-hand edge of field, then through gate and continue up valley alongside wood. Just before far corner, turn right through gate onto sunken fenced path. Follow this up to gate beside house, then left at junction of paths. Exit onto the road and turn right to return.

▲ *Dovecotes, like this one at Pauntley, were used to breed pigeons to provide fresh meat for the lean winter months.*

ALL PHOTOS PAUL FELIX

may have been built by the Whittingtons in the 1500s. In the grounds is a square stone dovecote.

The church **A** is Norman in origin and has a magnificent chancel arch with two rows of zig-zag mouldings or 'chevrons'. Be sure also to go around the outside to look at the 12th-century south doorway. Here is another chevroned arch enclosing a tympanum (the space between a lintel and an arch), covered in a fish-scale design. The side chapel was built by the Whittingtons around 1430. The church has been recently restored, with assistance from the Lord Mayor of London.

Perhaps the highlight of the walk is the section along the Leadon near Durbridge Farm, where the river cuts through the sandstone hills to create a little known but remarkably beautiful small gorge, with hanging woods and old farm buildings.

Much of the shaping of this area happened during the Ice Age, which ended about 20,000 years ago. Tongues of ice from the Welsh mountains blocked many of the existing river valleys to create large lakes from which the water found new routes out to sea, the largest of which is the Ironbridge Gorge on the Severn below Shrewsbury.

WIDE VALLEYS

Immediately after the Ice Age, the floods of melt-water caused many rivers to cut much deeper channels on their existing courses. The detailed history of the area at this time is still unclear, but traces of ice erosion remain in both the wide, smooth-sided valleys, which may be former courses of the river, and the main valley of the Leadon.

The combination of the bending river, the hanging woods and the vivid red sandstone creates some

▲*Durbridge Mill and the adjoining oast house is a magnificent old stone building. From the excellent vantage point of Durbridge Farm (left), you have a fine view down along the gorge, where the River Leadon is edged with trees.*

▲*The Three Choirs Vineyard at harvest time. The wines produced are similar in character to white German wines.*

spectacular scenery. Coming down a side valley, you pass between woods containing oak, beech and holly, and a lake **B** fringed with bulrushes and, in summer, covered in waterlilies. A section along the slow-flowing Leadon brings you to Durbridge Farm **C**, where there is a fine view of the gorge, with the river flowing below between rows of trees.

IDYLLIC MILL

Durbridge Mill **D** is a vision out of a Constable landscape: old buildings blending into the landscape; an oast house built of sandstone; a stream running beneath the buildings and a mill wheel, disused but still in place. You climb out of the valley to the sandstone plateau, with a magnificent view over the River Leadon.

Soon after the Leadon Gorge, the

◀*The present Pauntley Court stands on the site of the original medieval Whittington family home.*

The Legend of a Lord Mayor

The real Dick Whittington was not the fairy-tale boy with the cat, but the 'last of the great mayors' of London. One of the most prosperous merchants of medieval England, he lent his ready money to kings on a princely scale and did good works in the city.

Richard Whittington was born at Pauntley some time in the 1350s and may indeed have walked to London, but not because he was an orphan. He was his father's third son and the family were going through a bad patch, but even so, he was not much more than 20 years old when he was first recorded as loaning money to the city authorities. From then on there is ample evidence of his prosperity, trading mainly in high quality cloth, including 'cloth of gold'. When the mayor of the city died in office in June 1397, the King appointed Whittington to succeed him. He was formally elected by the Aldermen in October of that year and again in 1406 and 1419.

He died in 1423, at a great age by the standards of the times. He had lent money to both Henry IV and Henry V and had been put in charge of expenses for the completion of Westminster Abbey. His wife, Alice, had died before him and they had no children, so he left his fortune to charity — to the modernisation of Newgate Prison, the founding of a

The real Sir Richard Whittington was a successful merchant, not a poor orphan boy who answered the call of Bow Bells.

library and a hospital, and the installation of a public water tap in Cripplegate; he is also believed to have helped with the repair of Gloucester Cathedral.

These and other projects endeared him to the common people and over time Sir Richard Whittington became a legendary figure, the legend being embellished with church bells and a trusty cat.

walk passes through part of the Three Choirs Vineyard. The Welsh borders may seem an unlikely spot for wine growing, but a 12th-century writer, commenting on Gloucestershire, stated that 'no county in England has so many or so good vineyards. The wines do not offend the mouth with sharpness, since they do not yield to the French in sweetness'. The Three Choirs Vineyard was established in 1973 and named after the festival of music linking Gloucester, Hereford, and Worcester Cathedrals. It is one of the six largest in Britain, covering

some 20 acres (8 hectares). You will notice that the vineyards are only on the south-facing slopes of the hills, with apple orchards behind.

NATIVE WINES

If you detour slightly you can visit the winery **E**, which is open on weekdays throughout the year and on Saturdays and Sundays between Easter and Christmas.

A guided tour of the winery can be made by arrangement and it is possible to taste and buy the wines, which are mostly white and Germanic in character. The shop also sells a tempting array of other local produce, including rounds of authentic Single and Double Gloucestershire cheese.

A WOODLAND TRAIL

modern forestry plantation of Mailscot Wood, falling away towards the River Wye below; a slight detour here leads to a viewpoint **D**, where you can see across to the cliffs and caves on the far side. A waymarked trail leads eventually to the lookout point of the Gated Rock: from here, you can look down to the river on either side. The Wye flows out of a gorge to your left, loops through the relatively low ground north of the Rock, and then turns

▲*Coldwell Rocks may have been named after this 'cold well' in the depths of the forest. The peregrine falcon (inset) watches for prey on woodland crags.*

PAUL FELIX. INSET:ROGER HOSKING:E & D HOSKING

FACT FILE

- English Bicknor, Forest of Dean, 3 miles (4.8 km) north of Coleford

- Outdoor Leisure Map 14, grid reference SO 582152

  miles 0 1 2 3 4 5 6 7 8 9 10 miles
  kms 0 1 2 3 4 5 6 7 8 9 10 11 12 13 14 15 kms

- Allow 3 hours

- Some woodland sections may be muddy after rain, so walking shoes are recommended

- **P** Roadside parking at entrance to English Bicknor church; car park at entrance to English Bicknor school, on right 150 yards (135 metres) along B4228 towards Berry Hill

- Rock Inn (food, garden) at Hillersland; snack counter at Symond's Yat Rock

- **WC** At Symond's Yat Rock

A walk above a gorge and forest to a rocky viewpoint

The walk begins in English Bicknor, one of the least industrial villages of the Forest of Dean; the village church has a fine Norman interior, although the outside is unremarkable. It was built in the outer courtyard of a Norman castle, and the mound on which the central keep lay can be seen just south of the church **A**. Leaving English Bicknor you get a good view of the high plateau lands of the Forest of Dean, and the farm buildings across the valley. Moving up the valley, you go through the secluded woods of Brooks Head Grove **B**, and then over farmland to rise to the highest point of the walk, from where there are fine views **C** north across the Herefordshire plain, and west to the Black Mountains.

The path then descends to the

▶ *This tombstone, with its decorative carved head, lies in the graveyard of St Mary's Church.*

PAUL FELIX

THE WALK

ENGLISH BICKNOR

The walk begins at the lychgate of English Bicknor church **A**.

1 Turn right and continue for 40 yards (36 metres), then go left on a road signposted to Eastbach Church Hill. At the bottom of the valley, go right over stile, then left across field to stile at right end of row of trees. Cross the second field to the stile at middle of far side, and continue across the third field which narrows to a point. Follow clear path through wood **B**, crossing clearing to a second wood.

2 Go through the right of two gates and keep close to right-hand edge of field; enter next field by gate/stile, then keep to right as path becomes rough track, passing barn on left. Go through gate, then keep close to hedge on right to reach road.

3 Cross the road to stile, then go diagonally left across field. Go over stile at far left corner, then uphill alongside fence to stile. Turn right on road for 40 yards (36 metres), then left over the stile, keeping close to the fence on right, where there are panoramic views **C**.

Continue into the second field, then through gate between farm buildings. Keep right to follow metalled access road; on reaching Hillview, fork right to reach major road and turn right.

4 Opposite the entrance to Folly Lane, 50 yards (45 metres) before the Rock Inn, turn left through vehicle barrier on the track into the wood, then after 30 yards (27 metres) go right on crossing path. Pass to the right of the enclosure and around Mailscot Lodge; avoid vehicle track to right and continue left and downhill on footpath. At the junction of tracks by the oak tree, 300 yards (270 metres) after the Lodge, keep right (detour left for viewpoint **D**). Ignore red waymarks, and ¼ mile (400 metres) later fork left. Soon cross a gravel vehicle track, and continue forward on path to left of bungalow, then alongside road and car park. From snack counter, go right over footbridge then left on path between fences to reach viewpoint.

5 Return along path but avoid footbridge, continuing forward with

road on right. When the wooden fence on the left ends, bear left on the path alongside wire fence, leading to a view of Goodrich church **E**. Bear right, still with wire fence on left, to car park. Continue towards metalled road ahead, but after 25 yards (22 metres), turn left through gap in bushes and continue downhill on path, passing sign saying 'No climbing on Coldwell Rocks'. Pass an old well **F** on your right.

6 Bear left and go over fixed metal gate. Continue ahead over rise, then take the left fork leading to a view of the woods below **G**. Be sure to remain

above the rock pinnacles, getting closer to the fence on the right. About 50 yards (45 metres) after metal gate on your right, go over stile into field. Continue forward and uphill, then make for stile beside large waymark arrow. Cross next field to stile in far right corner, then go downhill to road. Turn right, then left at junction. After cottages, go left through gate into recreation ground and follow the hedge on left, into playground. Go down the footpath between right corner of main school building and railing, to enter the churchyard through the gate.

▲ *Wide views over open farmland follow the wooded seclusion of Brook's Head Grove.*

south through another gorge, cutting through the high lands of the plateau. It is believed that the great looping meanders of the river were formed when the landscape was much flatter; then, as the rocks forming the plateau were pushed slowly upwards, the river cut down into them to maintain its route.

HOLY WELL

From the Gated Rock, the path takes you along the cliffs passing another viewpoint, where you can see as far north as Goodrich church **E**. Descending into the woods, you reach a spring emerging into an old stone stoup (a small basin for holy water) **F**: this is perhaps the 'cold well' which gave its name to the rocks in this section.

Nearing the end of the walk, you look down through the woods from another viewpoint **G**. Abundant yew trees seem almost to hang suspended above the river. The many limestone pinnacles contain the nesting sites of peregrine falcons; they are protected by the Royal Society for the Protection of Birds, and information about them is available at the Gated Rock.

STANTON AND SNOWSHILL

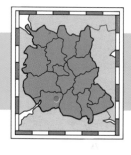

◄ *The garden at Snowshill Manor is spectacular when in full bloom. In the foreground is a Venetian well-head. The wood mouse (inset) is common in gardens and throughout the countryside.*

MIKE WILLIAMS/NATIONAL TRUST PHOTOGRAPHIC LIBRARY. INSET: PAUL STERRY/NATURE PHOTOGRAPHERS LTD

St Michael and All the Angels **A**. The church has a Perpendicular exterior, with a pretty spire, but parts of the interior date from the earlier Norman period. The Victorian restorer, Sir Ninian Cowper, designed many of the furnishings. The walk continues along the main street of Stanton **B** which has been described as 'architecturally...the most distinguished of the smaller villages in the Cotswolds'.

LOOKING TO A FOLLY

From Stanton, you climb fairly steeply up the Cotswold scarp, through attractive woods with many horse chestnut trees. From the ancient settlement at Shenberrow Hill **C** there is a magnificent view over Stanton to the farmlands of the Severn plain, with Bredon Hill prominent in the middle distance. Later you have good views **D** over the Cotswold plateau; Snowshill village nestles into the side of a hill, while Broadway Tower, a folly, is prominent on the skyline beyond it.

The village of Snowshill **E** is notable for its traditional cottages in mellow Cotswold stone, its setting, with fine views over the Severn Valley, and its history. Snowshill

▼ *High on a hill to the north-east of Snowshill stands Broadway Tower, a folly built in 1797 by Lady Coventry.*

Through panoramic hills to two old Cotswold villages

This walk links two beautiful and historic Cotswold villages. Most of it is along footpaths and bridleways through woodlands and open countryside, with views over the market gardens of the Vale of Evesham to the Welsh hills.

It starts in the quietly attractive village of Laverton, then follows a straightforward path through fields at the foot of the Cotswold escarpment to Stanton. The village is entered through the churchyard of

FACT FILE

🌞 Laverton, just off the B4632 (former A46), 2 miles (3 km) south-west of Broadway

📰 Pathfinder 1043 (SP 03/13), grid reference SP 074356

```
miles 0  1  2  3  4  5  6  7  8  9  10 miles
kms 0 1 2 3 4 5 6 7 8 9 10 11 12 13 14 15 kms
```

◔ Allow 3½ to 4 hours

▭ One steep ascent from Stanton; Laverton-Stanton section may be muddy after rain

P On-street parking at start of walk

🍺🍴 The Mount Inn in Stanton and The Snowshill Arms in Snowshill

🏰 Snowshill Manor open April–October at weekends, 11–1 and 2–6; May–September open Wed–Mon. Admission fee

PAUL FELIX

THE WALK

LAVERTON – STANTON – SNOWSHILL

The walk begins outside the Post Office in Laverton.

1 Go downhill, passing side road on right, then turn left following footpath sign. Following wall/fence on left by garden, cross several stiles to reach road.

2 Turn left, then right after 40 paces over stile into field. Just before far left corner, go left then immediately right over stiles and follow hedge on right. After next stile, turn immediately left around head of field, then down side. Maintain direction over two more stiles, but at far corner of next field bear left over stile, avoiding stream ahead. Follow hedge on right for 100 yards (90m), then go right over footbridge and through metal gate onto fenced path. After sharp right turn, enter churchyard. Keep left of church **A**, then right down lane.

3 Go left up village street **B**, forking left after phone box. After passing Mount Inn continue uphill on track between two car parks. In first field follow fence on right to gate into second field. Bear away from fence towards gate, then in third field continue forward, ignoring tracks, towards waymark post to left of projecting corner of wood. Inside wood, keep just to

left of sunken way leading to waymark by ruined barn.

4 Keep left of barn, then at next waymark turn right on track; beyond barn, take uphill fork following fence on right. Continue through stone gateposts, now with fence on left. On reaching wall ahead, go left over stile and steeply uphill beside wall to reach track. Turn right through gate then left. At top of rise, turn right to marker post and settlement **C**; bear left to cross dip ahead to Shenberrow Buildings.

5 Follow waymark through gate to left of buildings to join track from farm. At signpost turn right on bridleway going around far side of buildings, and at next signpost turn left, over brow of hill. After gate, turn left on track for 30 paces (good views here **D**) then bear half-right across field towards gate in far side. Continue across second field, then through gate onto metalled

lane descending towards Snowshill village; at junction, turn left on road to enter village **E**.

6 Retrace steps to leave village, but after last house on right go through gate and downhill on farm road. Follow this through second gate, but at next gate stay inside field, following hedge. Go over stile at corner, then follow hedge on right. Go through gate-stile, then forward across field, making for gate to left of farm buildings.

7 Turn left on farm road for 20 paces, then sharp right on track above buildings (vista to north **F**).

Continue until track turns sharply left.

8 Go left through gate (good views here **G**), aiming midway between obvious track downhill and wood on left. Once visible, make for stile in wooden fence. Turn left before it on path inside fence.

9 At corner go through gate onto fenced track but after 100 yards (90m) turn right through gate onto track, with fence on left. Initially level, this track steepens and becomes sunken; follow track through two gates, then down Laverton's main street to the starting point.

Manor, owned by the National Trust, originally belonged to the great Benedictine abbey at Winchcombe. It was seized in 1539 by Henry VIII, who gave it to his sixth and last wife, Catherine Parr. The house is now remarkable for a collection of furniture and other antiques, the garden, and the build-

ing itself, a typical Cotswold manor house with parts dating from c1500.

From Snowshill, you drop down into a valley and there is a good view back up towards the village. As you pass Great Brockhampton Farm, there is a magnificent vista **F** down the valley, through a parkland landscape to the much larger village

of Broadway and the fields of the Vale of Evesham beyond.

Finally, as you turn west towards Laverton, a new view **G** along the scarp to the south-west opens up, with Bredon Hill to the north-west, while below you is the village of Buckland, with its golden church full of architectural treasures.

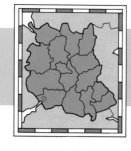

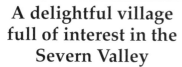

A delightful village full of interest in the Severn Valley

Frampton on Severn is a rare example of a working village with many attractive buildings. It is wholly unspoilt; apart from a small chocolate factory, the only industries here have been farming, some quarrying for gravel, and the production of cider and perry.

The village is almost surrounded by water, with gravel pit lakes to the east and a canal to the west, in addition to the two rivers from which its name derives. Frampton is a corruption of Frometon, and the Frome curves round the village to meet the Severn, which flows just to the west.

The heart of the village is its 20-acre (8.1-hectare) green **Ⓐ**, the longest in the county. A road runs down the middle, but there is still ample room for a cricket pitch, three ponds and grazing animals. Along it are half-timbered buildings, stone Georgian villas and some 19th-century brick cottages with tile or stone roofs.

Nearly every style of vernacular English architecture is on view. Five of the cottages have cruck frames, a primitive form of half-timbering where whole oak trees were split down the middle and jointed to support the framework at each end.

15TH-CENTURY FARMHOUSE

The most distinguished timber-framed building on the green is Manor Farm **Ⓑ**, built on the site of a Norman lord's manor in the 15th century, when a large barn and dovecote were added. Jane Clifford, who was a mistress of Henry II and reputedly poisoned by agents of Eleanor of Aquitaine, was born in the manor about 1140.

A footpath leads from the green to The Gloucester and Sharpness Canal **Ⓒ**, completed in 1831. This ship canal could take vessels up to 600 tons, more than any other canal, and took pressure off the

▲*The ornamental canal leading to the Gothic orangery at Frampton Court. The snow goose (above left) is a scarce winter visitor from arctic America and Greenland that feeds with other geese.*

◀*This 15th-century half-timbered barn, with a brick and stone base, is at Manor Farm. It is rather unusual in having square panels instead of oblong ones.*

FACT FILE

- Frampton on Severn, 8 miles (12.8km) south-west of Gloucester, on the B4071

- Pathfinder 1112 (SO 70), grid reference SO 749081

  miles 0 1 2 3 4 5 6 7 8 9 10 miles
  kms 0 1 2 3 4 5 6 7 8 9 10 11 12 13 14 15 kms

- Allow about 2½ hours

- Level walking suitable for the whole family. Small children should be supervised on the canal section

- **P** On the street by the green

- **T** Hourly bus service from Gloucester

- The Bell pub and The Three Horseshoes pub, both in Frampton

- **I** Manor Farm and Frampton Court have occasional open days; for details of these, and other tourist information, Tel. (01452) 421188

THE WALK

FRAMPTON ON SEVERN

The walk starts by the post office near the north end of the green **A**.

1 ➡ Walk down the western side of the green to Manor Farm **B**, and turn right on the footpath beside it, signposted to Frampton Bridge. Follow the waymarked path across fields to the canal **C**.

2 ➡ Turn right along the towpath to a swingbridge **D**. Cross it and turn left to follow the towpath, signposted 'The Severn Way', to Splatt Bridge.

3 ➡ Cross it and follow the path left along the canal bank to the church **E**. Continue to the Avenue. Go straight ahead, through a lych gate, and carry on up The Street. Take the first turning right as you approach the green. Continue on this leafy lane for about 300 yards (270m) to where a footpath crosses it, with a boathouse on your right.

4 ➡ Cross the stile on your left and follow waymark arrows across a field, past a large oak tree in its centre, to the fishponds **F**.

5 ➡ Bear left, keeping the water on your right. Pass a cottage on your right and make for a stile in the far corner of the field. Cross into a lane and go over the stile opposite. Follow the footpath into the grounds of Frampton Court **G** to view the house and ponds.

6 ➡ Walk back to the lane. Turn right and follow it back to the green. Turn right past the west entrance to Frampton Court, then cross the green to the start.

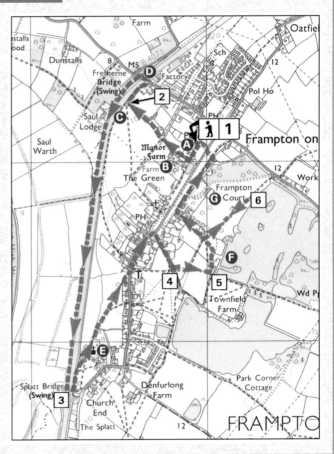

Severn at the height of the Industrial Revolution. The swingbridge keepers' cottages **D**, with their Doric columns and porticos, reflect the great commercial success of the canal. The towpath is now part of the Severn Way.

From Splatt Bridge, the walk leads to the Church of St Mary the Virgin **E**, consecrated in 1305. There is a rare and ancient lead font inside, as well as monuments to local families. A charming feature is a swallows' nest above the front porch lamp, which has been there as long as anyone can remember.

You return to the village along the Avenue, one of the joys of Frampton. Mature chestnut trees shade an unpaved path leading to a stone-roofed lych gate onto The Street, below the green. A lane leads to the fishponds **F**, dug to provide material for the banks of the canal. Now naturalized, these old gravel pits are very popular with fishermen and wildfowl alike.

GAGGLES OF GEESE

The route enters the 18th-century parkland of Frampton Court **G**, where lush grass, once cropped by cattle and thoroughbred horses, fattens gaggles of wild geese. In winter, white-fronted, pink-footed and snow geese waddle about, while Canada geese predominate in the summer months.

The elegant court itself was built between 1731 and 1733 by a local architect who borrowed heavily from the work of Hawksmoor and Vanbrugh. Its first owner, Richard Clutterbuck, was a self-made man of some wealth and taste. He had the swamp beside his house drained to create the green, and later added an upright Gothic villa, to serve as an orangery, and an ornamental canal in the Dutch style.

Tantalizing glimpses of the house can be had over a high brick boundary wall or through the splendid wrought-iron gates on your return to the green, but the best view — unless you visit on a rare open day — is across the grounds from the path by the fishponds.

The presence of the canal and ponds meant that aquatic plants became a feature of the gardens. Generations of ladies from the Clutterbuck family and their successors, the Cliffords, passed the time drawing them. Their sketch-books and portfolios, discovered in the attic, have since been published as a book, entitled *Frampton's Flora*.

ROGER VLITOS

◄ *The walk runs alongside the canal to Fretherne Bridge, a swingbridge.*

STONE, GLASS AND GRAVEL

RAY GRANGER. INSET: LUTRA/NHPA

▲*Converted now to a house, Fairford's 17th-century water-mill is built of Cotswold limestone, like most of the buildings in the area. The dace (inset) swims in the River Coln. St Mary's Church (below right) has an elegant exterior but its chief glories are inside.*

Fine buildings and a waterfowl haven in a small Cotswold town

Two factors above all others gave the towns and villages of the Cotswolds their characteristic look: stone and sheep. The hard, fine-grained oolitic limestone that forms the Cotswold bedrock makes excellent building stone, while the trade in wool, England's premier export in the late Middle Ages, brought great wealth to the area.

Much of this wealth went into the building of country houses and churches, as well as streets full of humbler buildings in the golden local stone. Fairford is typical; its main country house is gone, but it compensates with a magnificent church. The town also has many attractive water features, some natural, some man-made, in the surrounding countryside.

FACT FILE

✴ Fairford, 7½ miles (12km) east of Cirencester, on the A417

▭ Pathfinder 1114 (SP 00/10), grid reference SP 152010

miles 0 1 2 3 4 5 6 7 8 9 10 miles
kms 0 1 2 3 4 5 6 7 8 9 10 11 12 13 14 15 kms

◐ Allow 2 hours

▭ Level walking on good paths and pavements. May be muddy by the lake and river in winter

P In the Market Place or outside the church; free car park at junction of Park Street and High Street

🍴 Several pubs, hotels and tea-rooms in Fairford

WC In the High Street near the church

The old centre of the town is the Market Place **Ⓐ**, where there are two old inns, the George and the Bull. The old road linking London and Cirencester runs across one end. From the other, the short High Street leads past the old school, which was built in 1738, to St Mary's Church **Ⓑ**.

There are many fine table-tombs of the 17th and 18th centuries in the churchyard, and a smaller, but no

RAY GRANGER

THE WALK

FAIRFORD

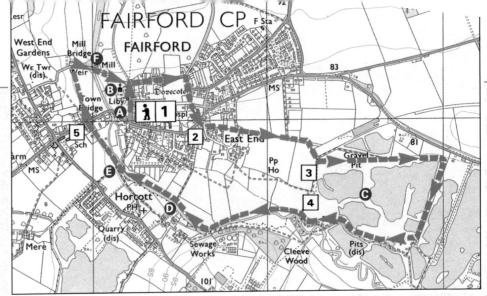

The walk begins outside the Bull Hotel in Fairford's Market Place **Ⓐ**.

1 ▶ Go north up the High Street, away from the main A417 road, passing the church **Ⓑ** on your left. At the end, turn right down Park Street. Follow the road round to the right. When it bends left, go straight on. At the next left bend, go through an opening in the stone wall ahead, and down a narrow alley. At the end, cross the road and continue ahead, walking past the Eight Bells pub on your left.

2 ▶ Turn left down Beaumoor Place. Where the road bends right, continue ahead down an alley, and over a step-stile into a field. Continue along the field edge, with a stone wall to your left, to another step-stile. Cross, and continue on a narrow path ahead. Where this widens out at a junction, go straight ahead through a gate, towards the lake **Ⓒ**.

3 ▶ Go down to the lake, and walk with the water on your right. At the end of the lake, turn right on a wide, grassy path. Bear right around a shingle beach, and follow the obvious path ahead, still keeping the water on your right. Where the path divides at the lake's end, go straight on towards some trees. Cross a footbridge to the River Coln **Ⓓ**.

4 ▶ Turn right and follow the river-bank through fields, then past gardens. Just after you pass a house on the opposite bank, go ahead through a small wooden gate and turn left over Dilly's Bridge **Ⓔ**. On the far bank, turn right and follow the tarmac path ahead, to a stone stile. Climb over this, and continue ahead down a lane to a main road.

5 ▶ Cross with care and follow the signposted footpath ahead, over a stone stile, then a wooden stile, into a field. Continue ahead, with a leat running on your right, to another stone stile. Cross, and turn right along the road, past the mill **Ⓕ** and the church, to the High Street. Turn right to return to the start.

---

less affecting, stone dedicated to Tiddles, the church cat. The church was built around 1500. A well proportioned building in the Perpendicular style, it is covered with exuberant decorative carving, including some fine grotesques. The church's finest feature is its stained glass. Contemporary with the church, it is the fullest, finest set of medieval stained glass surviving in any English parish church.

Some windows tell Bible stories, from Eden to the Ascension; the glittering images illustrated the scriptures for a largely illiterate congregation. Others contain portraits of saints, martyrs and apostles. The huge west window pictures the Day of Judgement. The top, heavenly, half is a 19th-century restoration, but the lower part, which depicts the Harrowing of Hell in rich red tones, is original.

From the church, the route leads up Park Street, named after Fairford Park, a 17th-century mansion that was demolished in the 1950s. All that remains today is a Victorian Gothic lodge and the landscaped grounds. A school was built on the mansion site in the 1960s.

GRAVEL PIT LAKE

A walk through the newer part of town leads into open country. Gravel was once dug here, and the old workings are now a water park. Several pits have filled with water, and now form a lake **Ⓒ**. Damselflies and dragonflies abound, and the shingly beaches and islands provide nesting places not only for the usual mallard, moorhens, coots and Canada geese, but also for oyster-catchers and common terns.

You walk round the lake, then return to Fairford along the bank of the River Coln **Ⓓ**, a clear, shallow stream, full of fish and water-crowfoot, that runs off the limestone to join the infant Thames. Dilly's Bridge **Ⓔ**, a wooden footbridge dedicated to the memory of a golden retriever, makes an excellent vantage point for watching the swans cruise by, or a female mallard fussing over a brood of ducklings.

A leat-side path running west of the village centre affords a fine view of the church across the fields, and leads to the restored 17th-century mill **Ⓕ** and its handsome millpond. A weir and an ornamental stone bridge on the far side of the pond mark the southern end of Broad Water, an artificial lake in the grounds of Fairford Park, made by damming the Coln. The church, High Street and the starting point of the walk are just a short way ahead.

◀ Shepherded by adults, a creche of Canada geese – birds from several broods – paddle across the gravel pits.

FACT FILE

✳ Stonor, Oxfordshire, off the B480, 5 miles (8 km) north of Henley-on-Thames

⌦ Pathfinders 1137 (SU 69/79) and Explorer 3, grid reference SU 737889

miles 0   1   2   3   4   5   6   7   8   9   10 miles
kms 0   1   2   3   4   5   6   7   8   9   10   11   12   13   14   15 kms

◔ Allow 3½ hours

▬ Too long and hilly for very small children and pushchairs

P Grass verge opposite Stonor Park

🍽 Stonor, Turville, Fingest

🏛 Stonor House. Open
I   31 March-29 September; Sun: 2-5pm; Mon, bank holidays only: 11am-5.30pm; Wed (May-Sept): 2-5.30pm; Sat (15 June-31 August): 2-5.30pm

▲The pretty brick-built cottages of Turville village. The brick ledges of these picturesque cottages are a favourite nesting place for the spotted flycatcher (left).

Off the beaten track in the Chilterns

This circular walk explores the less frequented hills and valleys of that beautiful stretch of beech-clad Downs, the Chilterns. It passes two remote villages with curious names, Turville and Fingest. Both are picturesque and each has a delightful village inn.

The walk starts from the deer park of Stonor **Ⓐ**, a gracious old house with some eight hundred years of history. Standing in a fold of a hill, the house and its 14th-century chapel are seen from the path through the beechwoods, across a narrow valley where deer still graze.

Soon after leaving the woods the county border between Oxfordshire

▶ Inside the porch of Turville village church, the list of the church's vicars extends back to 1228.

and Buckinghamshire is crossed. At the hamlet of Southend is an old inn, now converted into a private house — 'The Drover'. This was the former halting place of the sheep drovers who moved Stonor sheep down Drovers' Lane to the wharf at Henley-on-Thames 5 miles (8 km) away. Shortly after passing Southend Farm the high ground affords wide views over the surrounding wooded hills. Turville Mill **Ⓑ**, a weatherboarded smock

PAUL FELIX

THE WALK

STONOR PARK – TURVILLE – FINGEST

The walk begins at Stonor Park off the B480.

1 Enter Stonor Park **A** from the B480 by the iron swing gate and follow the public footpath ahead, uphill. Stonor House is in view to the left and the path rises above the valley. It is clearly marked by white arrows painted on trees. After passing through a gate in the deer fence, the path enters a wood and in about 100 yards (90 metres) joins a wider path. Continue straight ahead on the wider path, still marked by white arrows, to join a track with an open field to the left. Continue ahead, passing a cottage on the left, to a road.

2 Turn left in the road and in 150 yards (135 metres) turn right along another narrow road and continue to Southend Farm.

After passing the farm, enjoy the extensive view over the Oxfordshire countryside. Turville's famous 'smock' windmill **B** is visible slightly to the left of the line of the path. When the farm road swings right, continue ahead over a stile and follow the path straight across the field. It soon runs downhill to a stile beside a small spinney. Cross the stile, follow its wide path downhill to another stile into a field and follow the path down the left side of this field to a road. Cross the road to the path opposite, which crosses the middle of a large field to a narrow path, marked by a post, between hedges leading into Turville **C**. Cross the village street to the path opposite, between cottages, and after a few paces climb the stile in the wire fence on the right. Cross the small field diagonally to a second stile and continue diagonally

uphill across this larger field to another stile. Cross the stile and follow the path ahead with a barbed wire fence to the left and the valley to the right. When it reaches a small road, cross to the path opposite and continue ahead for a few paces, then follow it as it bends to the right to join the road at Fingest **D**.

3 Turn right in the road and, after a few paces, bear left along a road signposted Skirmett. Follow this road for almost 880 yards (800 metres) and turn right along a private drive marked with footpath sign. On reaching a stile, cross this and follow the path steeply uphill to Poynatts Wood. Follow the path around to the right and when it soon forks at a sign marked, bizarrely, 'Private, vermin control', fork right along the narrower lower path along the edge of the wood, with valley views to the right. On reaching a

second control sign turn right down a signposted path to cross a stile into a field. Cross the middle of this field to a path through a thicket to a road. Turn left in the road and in 50 yards (45 metres), when the road turns sharply right, take the bridleway on the left. It soon forks; keeping right, ignore all paths to the left and right, and continue ahead passing through a gate to enter a wood. Follow the track through a second gate for almost 1 mile (1.6 km). When this is joined by another track, continue ahead, ignoring paths to left and right to follow the track to Kimble Farm. Continue past the farm and follow the track around the left side of the pond to a road.

4 Turn right in the road and after 150 yards (135 metres) bear left along a single track road. Follow the road for just over 880 yards

◄*The well-maintained, black-sailed windmill on top of the ridge behind Turville village was featured extensively in the 1968 film* Chitty Chitty Bang Bang. *When you reach the summit of the ridge, the view from the windmill (right) is one of the finest of the Chiltern Hills.*

mill is prominent on the hill ahead. Smock mills were developed in the 1600s. These mills were fitted with a revolving cap to which the sails were fixed, together with a fantail mechanism: the fan automatically

turned the cap so that the sails always faced into the wind.

Descending through fields, the village of Turville **C** is entered by way of a lane lined with old flint-faced cottages. The lane opens into

the middle of the village and here other cottages, with flower-filled gardens, huddle around the small village green. On one side is the village inn, the Bull and Butcher. Completing the scene on the other

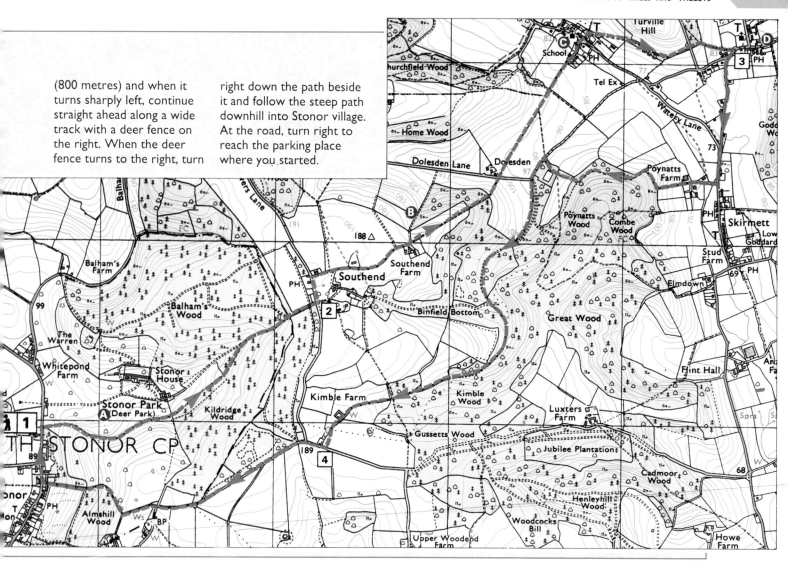

(800 metres) and when it turns sharply left, continue straight ahead along a wide track with a deer fence on the right. When the deer fence turns to the right, turn right down the path beside it and follow the steep path downhill into Stonor village. At the road, turn right to reach the parking place where you started.

side is the church with its massive squat Norman tower. (The name Turville derives from the Saxon Thyr-Feld or Thyri's field. The Normans had difficulty in pronouncing this and modified it to the French-sounding Turville.)

VILLAGE VIEW

Striking uphill towards the mill, a path branches to the right across the field and contours around the slope. The stile at the top offers a good place for a pause and a glance back down to the village, neat and compact in the little valley between the rolling hills.

A little further around the wooded hill another view unfolds, of a valley running southwards towards the Thames. The path continues between a thick screen of trees to emerge, most abruptly, in the village of Fingest **D**.

The village's most striking feature is its unusual church tower,

which is crowned by a double gable. Opposite is the well-preserved 17th-century Chequers Inn. Like Turville, Fingest is an ancient village; its name suggests it was once an important meeting place. Formerly

▶ *Note the unusual double saddleback roof of the Fingest parish church. The inside of the Norman tower is so large that it may originally have been the nave where the members of the congregation sat, with the present church's small nave probably being the site of the original chancel.*

spelt Tynghyrst, it means 'wooded hill of assembly'.

A short distance along the lane is Skirmett. Its Danish place name has a similar meaning: 'Shire meeting place'. From the outskirts of

PAUL FELIX

Skirmett, an ascent is made into the wooded hills above the village. Once the trees are reached, a level path circles Poynatts Wood. Through the trees the converging valleys are spread out below. A broad forest track that descends into one of these valleys is followed for over 1 mile (1.6 km) through the splendid Great Wood. Emerging from the wood and passing Kimple Farm, extensive views to the south over the distant Thames unfold. Soon the deer park is reached and a steep path descends through the trees to Stonor village.

◀ *The footpath continues past Kimble Farm, after which there are extensive views over the distant Thames.*

A Catholic Refuge

The Stonor family have lived in Stonor House for over 800 years, each generation adding to the medieval core, the aisled hall. The present 'E' shape dates from the 16th century.

During Elizabethan times when Catholics suffered under penal laws and were suspected of being traitors, Stonor was a centre of Catholicism and Mass continued to be celebrated in the Chapel of the Blessed Trinity that was built next to the house in 1349. In 1580, Edmund Campion, an English Jesuit, was sent on a mission to England. He preached in the area around Stonor and lived in secret in the house. In a hidden room in the roof he supervised the printing of his book *Decem Rationes* (The ten

reasons for being a Catholic) and he distributed 400 copies in St Mary's, Oxford, before the degree-giving ceremony on 27 June 1581.

The following month, while preaching at Lyford, Berkshire, he was arrested by a spy, George Eliot, and taken to the Tower. There he was put on the rack but refused to renounce his faith, although he swore loyalty to Elizabeth.

Before his execution on December 1, he wrote: 'If our religion do make us traitors we are worthy to be condemned, but otherwise we are and have been good subjects as ever the queen had.' Edmund Campion was beatified (declared by the Pope to be blessed in Heaven) in 1886.

Stonor Park was a Catholic stronghold after the Reformation. The 16th-century Jesuit martyr Edmund Campion had a secret room there, which hid a printing press. Other contents include fine bronzes and a shell-shaped bed supported by mermaids. In the grounds, fallow deer graze.

Nature walk

MALE FALLOW DEAR shed their antlers and grow new (larger) ones yearly. At eight years old the antlers reach full size.

In May, scabs form where the antlers are shed.

In July, the nascent antlers begin to branch.

By August, the antlers have reached full size.

In late August, the protective antler skin is shed in bloody strips, leaving the antlers pristine.

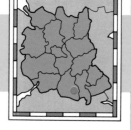

24

A walk through a nature reserve in a deeply incised gorge

The noise and rush of the A34 contrast with the peace and tranquillity of the path up Happy Valley **C** through Chilswell Copse. The trunk road now divides the village of South Hinksey from its hinterland, but then Matthew Arnold, the Victorian poet and literary critic, who often walked these paths, observed that 'in the two Hinkseys nothing keeps the same'. The same old inspiring view of Oxford can be seen from the descending path, however.

The General Eliott **A** is a pub named after General John Eliott, who relieved Gibraltar in September 1782, after it had been besieged for two years by the Spaniards. The village of South Hinksey is a lot older

PAUL FELIX. INSET: MIKE READ/SWIFT PICTURE LIBRARY

FACT FILE

- South Hinksey, 1½ miles (2 km) south of Oxford

- Pathfinder 1116 (SP 40/50), grid reference SP 510042

```
miles 0   1   2   3   4   5   6   7   8   9   10 miles
kms  0  1 2 3 4 5 6 7 8 9 10 11 12 13 14 15 kms
```

- Allow 2 hours

- One gradual climb and descent. Lanes, field and woodland paths, which may be muddy. Walking shoes recommended

- **P** The General Eliott, South Hinksey

- The General Eliott

- **T** Very infrequent bus service (no. 104 Oxford-Boars Hill) stops near the bridge over the A34 at South Hinksey. Or start from Hinksey swimming pool, which is served by frequent buses using Oxford's Abingdon Road; take path over footbridge across lakes and railway to reach South Hinksey near The General Eliott pub

than that. It may even derive its name from Hengist, the 5th-century Saxon leader who was invited to defend the British king, Vortigern. Hengist's brother Horsa may have given his name to Horspath, to the east of Oxford. These Saxons soon turned on the British, invited their compatriots over from Germany and pressed up the Thames valley. The Corallian limestone hills above would have been held by the Britons, making this a frontier zone in Arthurian times.

THE REEDBEDS

The oldest building to be seen in South Hinksey is St Lawrence church **B**. Parts of this building date from the 13th century, while the base of a 15th-century cross can be seen in the churchyard.

The nature reserve of Happy

▲ *Wood anemones bloom in spring in the deciduous woodlands of the Happy Valley. The carrion crow (right) is a wary and often quite solitary bird.*

Valley **C** was eroded when the force of water was much greater than that trickling down the stream today. The board walk takes you through a rare example of reedbeds, since others in Oxfordshire have been 'improved' by draining to allow agricultural use. The reedbeds here provide a habitat for reed bunting and sedge warbler, while birds (including stock dove and tawny owl) can be found in the woodland.

THE WALK

HAPPY VALLEY

The walk begins at The General Eliott Ⓐ, a pub in South Hinksey. This is just off the A34 to the south-west of Oxford.

1▶ Walk into the village and fork left along St Lawrence Road. Follow the road around a right- and then a left-hand bend to Church Close, passing St Lawrence church Ⓑ on your right. St Lawrence road continues to the right, round the end of the churchyard, and then becomes Parker Road.

2▶ Turn right along Parker Road. Ignore Manor Road on your right and go ahead to cross a bridge over the A34. Ignore a private road to Hinksey Hill Farm on your right but go ahead, beside the A34 on your left, along Chilswell Road.

3▶ Turn right, as signposted, up Chilswell Path. The Rambler's Jubilee Circular Walk footpath goes in this direction. Pass houses on your right, then ignore a bridge over a stream on your left (this leads to private property). Go ahead up the field path, walking parallel to power lines, which you will see 219 yards (200 metres) away to your right.

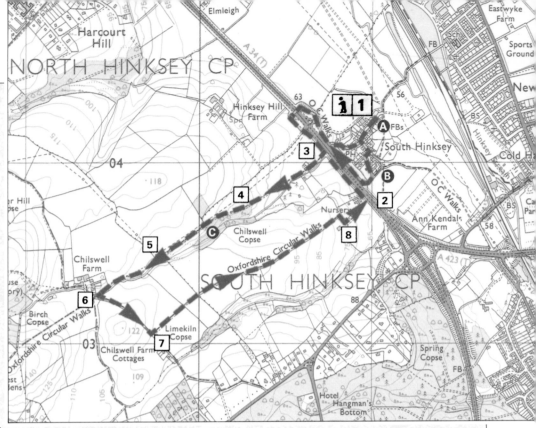

4▶ Bear left along a board walk through reeds. This leads to the oak woodland of Chilswell Copse and the nature reserve of Happy Valley Ⓒ. The boards end at the stream crossing, on entering the copse. Follow the path with a stream on your right (this path can be very slippery in wet weather). Cross tne stream again presently and go up the valley, through a clearing after the wood, to a stile in a corner beside an information board about the wildlife (ignoring the right fork leading up to a steep bank in the clearing beyond the wood).

5▶ Continue over the stile along a path with the stream on your left. Cross a track and walk beside a fence on your right to a signposted stile about 11 yards (10 metres) beyond the track.

6▶ Cross the stile into a worn tarmac lane and turn sharp left, away from Chilswell Farm. (Ignore the stile on the opposite side of the lane and the Rambler's Jubilee Circular Walk Bridleway close to it.) Follow this lane for 400 yards (360 metres).

7▶ About 164 yards (150 metres) before the large cottages on the right turn left down a signposted bridleway (which can be deep in mud). This goes through a small gate, then beside a hedge on your left. Go ahead through a hedge-gap and across a field. Continue through a gate and beside a hedge on your right. At the hedge and trees at the bottom of the hill follow the bridleway sharp right to join the access lane of Southcombe House.

8▶ Go left down the lane, past Johnson's Garden Centre on left, with the A34 close to the right, to recross bridge across the A34. Turn left along Manor Road back to the start.

In April and May you can enjoy the bluebells, while dog's mercury can be seen in February. Look for golden saxifrage in the stream. The oak trees are accompanied by ash and hazel, whose nuts are stored by squirrels in the autumn. In July marbled white butterflies can be seen fluttering through the woods.

BOTH PHOTOS: PAUL FELIX

◀ *The 16th-century, timber-framed and stone Horseshoe House has changed little since it was built. The base of a 15th-century cross (right) stands in St Lawrence's churchyard.*

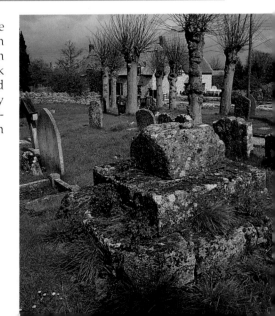

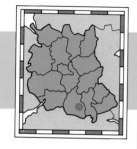

25

OXFORDSHIRE

A HILLTOP VILLAGE

CHRIS ANDREWS. INSET: STEPHEN DALTON/NHPA

A walk with fine views in the heart of Oxfordshire

▲ *The tower of St Mary's Church dates from 1160. Sited on a hill, the church offers panoramic views. The common wasp (right) is seen in late summer and autumn; it can sting several times.*

The Saxons chose a fine 'Gaerse dun' (grassy hill) to settle on. Forming the highest ridge between Oxford and the Chilterns, the hill provides views of the surrounding countryside. Until recently, this was an agricultural community, but now the car factories of Cowley beckon. However, this old village is a world away from such industry.

VILLAGE COMMUNITY

The Plough **Ⓐ** has been a focal point of the community since the 18th century. As late as the Enclosures Award of 1823, it was detailed as having an orchard and being owned by a baker. The wooden village hall dates from 1905, when the Morrell family built it. On the same side just after the hall is a house that served as a Methodist chapel until 1945.

Much of Garsington is owned by colleges of Oxford University; Library Farm, opposite the old chapel, has its rent collected in aid of the library of Exeter College. Opposite the 18th-century Red Lion are the Old Kennels which used to house Christ Church College's beagles. Garsington House **Ⓑ** was part of an estate owned by Exeter College in the 16th century.

In Garsington, look for owl holes **Ⓓ** in the buildings when you come to a road (Southend). Manor Farm Cottage (No 78) has one in its right-hand gable end, while No 93, the 16th-century farmhouse opposite it, has an owl hole high up in the left-hand gable. Owls were encouraged to nest by farmers wishing to keep down vermin.

If there is a hint of an ancient site in Garsington, it is the church of St Mary's **Ⓔ**. Cromwell's soldiers may have stabled their horses inside the church, whose tower dates from 1160. An interesting memorial is one to Thomas Radley, his wife and 10

FACT FILE

⚹ Garsington, Oxfordshire, 5 miles (3 km) south-east of Oxford

▭ Pathfinder 1116 (SP 40/50), grid reference SP 580022

miles 0 1 2 3 4 5 6 7 8 9 10 miles
kms 0 1 2 3 4 5 6 7 8 9 10 11 12 13 14 15 kms

◖ Allow 1½ hours

▬ Field paths and lanes. Overgrown in summer so wear stout shoes and thick trousers. Not suitable for small children in late spring when oilseed rape is at its full height.

Ⓟ Near the Plough, which has a small car park for patrons

Ⓣ Buses 101 and 103 (Oxford-Watlington)

THE WALK

GARSINGTON – DENTON

The walk begins at the Plough Ⓐ, in the centre of Garsington village.

1 With your back to the Plough, go left along Oxford Road, passing the village hall on your right. Continue past the Red Lion on your left and reach Garsington House Ⓑ on your right. The railed and elevated pavement divides here.

2 Bear right along the level part of the pavement to turn right through a small, waymarked gate. Follow a wall on your right to a waymarked stile. Go over it and continue to a broken but waymarked stile in the hedge opposite. Continue across the next field, over another stile and between gardens to a road.

3 Go right for 50 yards (45 metres) then turn left along a rough lane between houses. This is signposted as the public footpath to Denton and soon continues over a stile as a field path. Descend to cross another stile and walk beside a hedge on your right for 150 yards (135 metres). Turn right over a stile then immediately turn left to walk with the hedge now on your left.

4 Cross a stile and veer slightly right to a stile that leads to a footbridge over a stream, which may be dried up, then continue as waymarked. Reach the far corner, turn left over a stile and take the path to a lane.

5 Turn right to follow the lane past Denton House Ⓒ. Maintain your direction at a T-junction, then pass the road to Wheatley on your left. Go ahead towards Chippinghurst.

6 Turn right through a gate to cross a farmyard. Continue along a track. Cross the bottom of the next field to a stile facing you.

7 Cut across the field to a gap near the corner. Bear right to join a hedge at the corner and continue round the field keeping the hedge on your right. You will come to a ditch and a barbed wire fence that has been partially knocked down to maintain right of way. Cross with care and continue round to stone stile.

8 Go over stone stile, which brings you to a private road with a house and garden on your left. Continue to public road and turn left along the pavement for 150 yards (135 metres). (Notice the owl-holes Ⓓ.)

9 Turn right over a stile beside a gate and near a letter box. Bear right to a stile in the far corner. Go ahead with a fence on your right. Follow the waymarked path over a stile in the next corner and along an enclosed path to a field. Cross this to St Mary's church Ⓔ.

10 Leave the church by its lych gate and turn right down the road for a close view of the Gizzel (pond) and manor house Ⓕ on your right.

11 Retrace your steps past the church, now on your left, and pass the dovecote Ⓖ on your left. Reach the green and turn left back to the Plough.

---

children. Thomas died in 1484, which was approximately when the lych gate was erected. Outside there are splendid views. The Chilterns are away to the east, while the Wittenham Clumps can be seen across the Thames to the south.

ILLUSTRIOUS VISITORS

Field paths lead across the parish border to Denton House Ⓒ with its fine architecture. Going down Southend, notice the Gizzel or spring-fed pond on your right. Next to it is the manor house Ⓕ, which was rebuilt in the early 17th century. An earlier building on this site was owned by Geoffrey Chaucer's son, Thomas. D H Lawrence, Aldous Huxley, Virginia Woolf, Siegfried Sassoon, Maynard Keynes and Bertrand Russell were to meet here between 1915 and 1924. Their hosts were the Morrells, who built the terraced Italianate garden. The house, which has a fine staircase and panelling, is private, but the garden is open twice a year (see the annual booklet of the National Gardens Scheme for dates).

The square building in the garden on your left, near the top of Southend, is an 18th-century dovecote Ⓖ. The author Rider Haggard lived for two years in the Well House, when it was the rectory.

▶ *Lying next to the manor house in Garsington is the Gizzel — a spring-fed pond that originally provided the village with fresh water but now only serves visiting wildlife.*

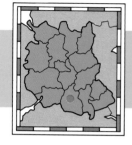

26

OXFORDSHIRE

CHRIS ANDREWS. INSET: STEPHEN DALTON/NHPA

▲*The River Ray at Islip follows its natural course; further on it has been straightened to facilitate drainage of Otmoor. The marsh fritillary (left) is found in wet meadows in early summer.*

FACT FILE

⁂ Islip, 5 miles (8 km) north of Oxford

⊡ Pathfinder 1092 (SP41/51), grid reference SP 527139

miles 0   1   2   3   4   5   6   7   8   9   10 miles
kms 0 1 2 3 4 5 6 7 8 9 10 11 12 13 14 15 kms

◐ Allow 3 hours

▭ Easy going, but muddy in wet weather. Some road walking, therefore not suitable for small children

P Swan Inn car park by river bridge

T Train from Oxford to Islip

▥ Islip and Noke

From the birthplace of a Saxon king and over the flatlands of Otmoor

This walk features the unusual wetland of Otmoor, with its rich and varied plant and bird life, quiet country lanes and three delightful Oxfordshire villages.

The walk begins in the village of Islip Ⓐ, a place which was once of considerable importance. There was a royal palace here in Saxon times, and it was the birthplace of Edward the Confessor. When he founded Westminster Abbey around 1050, he made it a present of 'ye little town' where he was born. The connection remained intact: the last Abbot of Westminster, when the monasteries were dissolved by Henry VIII, was an Islip man and the village rectors are still appointed by Westminster.

COACHING INNS

In later years, Islip was also an important stopping-off place on the main coaching route from London to Worcester. Of the many inns that served the trade, only two now survive and the walk begins opposite one of them, the Swan Inn. Islip was also the scene of a Civil War battle, and the inn is allegedly haunted by one of its victims — though the present landlord says he sleeps undisturbed by ghosts.

The first part of the walk takes you across the bridge over the River

THE WALK

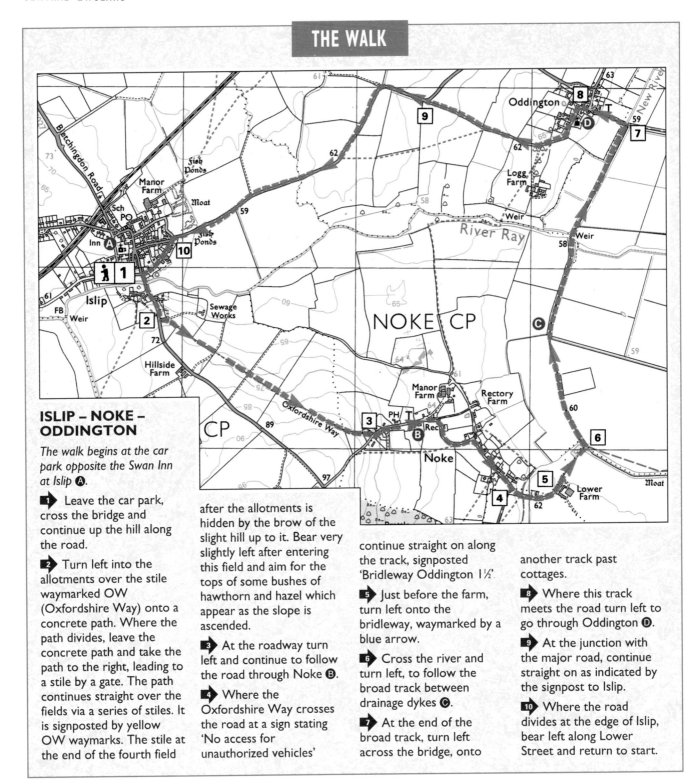

ISLIP – NOKE – ODDINGTON

The walk begins at the car park opposite the Swan Inn at Islip Ⓐ.

1 Leave the car park, cross the bridge and continue up the hill along the road.

2 Turn left into the allotments over the stile waymarked OW (Oxfordshire Way) onto a concrete path. Where the path divides, leave the concrete path and take the path to the right, leading to a stile by a gate. The path continues straight over the fields via a series of stiles. It is signposted by yellow OW waymarks. The stile at the end of the fourth field after the allotments is hidden by the brow of the slight hill up to it. Bear very slightly left after entering this field and aim for the tops of some bushes of hawthorn and hazel which appear as the slope is ascended.

3 At the roadway turn left and continue to follow the road through Noke Ⓑ.

4 Where the Oxfordshire Way crosses the road at a sign stating 'No access for unauthorized vehicles' continue straight on along the track, signposted 'Bridleway Oddington 1½'.

5 Just before the farm, turn left onto the bridleway, waymarked by a blue arrow.

6 Cross the river and turn left, to follow the broad track between drainage dykes Ⓒ.

7 At the end of the broad track, turn left across the bridge, onto another track past cottages.

8 Where this track meets the road turn left to go through Oddington Ⓓ.

9 At the junction with the major road, continue straight on as indicated by the signpost to Islip.

10 Where the road divides at the edge of Islip, bear left along Lower Street and return to start.

Ray. To the left the river wanders down between pollarded willows from the wastes of Otmoor, while to the right it runs past the gardens of village houses to the old water mill. It is a lovely spot, favoured by swans, geese and ducks. Beyond the bridge to the right is a group of cottages built of the warm local stone, one of which was home to the poet and novelist Robert Graves, who lived in the village in the years following World War I. For a short way, the walk goes uphill along the former coaching road, now reduced to B-road status. Looking back you get a view of the magnificent old Rectory, built in 1689 by Dr Robert South, rector of Islip, who founded the village school. The 15th-century church tower rises beyond it. Dr South also paid for the Church's restoration, but the Victorians have since made alterations.

The path now turns onto the Oxfordshire Way, which runs across a series of fields. In summer it is narrow, with waist-high corn on either side. From here you can look across the flat land of Otmoor, to the surrounding hills: not grand hills, but sufficiently high to allow settlements above the damp plain of the moor. This section of the walk ends in a lane, bordered by high hedges. Once this lane was an important one in the life of the community, for the church at Noke became united to that of Islip, and the people of Noke carried their dead across the fields for funerals.

TO OTMOOR

Noke ❷ is very unlike Islip. Where the latter is a tightly bunched village, set on a main road, Noke straggles out along a winding lane that eventually peters out on the edges of Otmoor. At first comes a

ALL PHOTOS CHRIS ANDREWS

▲ *The path through the corn fields is part of the Oxfordshire Way leading from Islip to Noke. Looking back towards Islip from the stile (below right) the 15th-century tower of the church of St Nicholas is visible in this predominantly flat landscape. The thatched cottage (left) is one of several that make Noke attractive to walk through before the contrast of the bleak moorland of Otmoor.*

road, Orchard Cottage, again with an ornate thatched roof that curves round little dormer windows.

Eventually the road leads into a bridleway, a broad green track, popular with walkers and riders, that takes you out onto Otmoor itself. At once you can see evidence of the effort that has gone into draining the moor. Overflow water is pumped from the river into a pond with an island in the middle, while the banks have been built up to contain the river itself. It seems quite a small stream, compared to the river first met at Islip, and the reason for that will appear later in the walk. The bridleway runs along a ridge, with the gentle river flowing through waving reeds on one side and thick-set hedge and ditch on the other.

MOOR DRAINAGE

Soon the pattern of Otmoor becomes plain, as a drainage ditch ❸ can be seen running straight and true at right angles to the river. This is the chequerboard of square fields, divided by hedges and ditches, described by an Oxford don, Charles Dodgson, better known as the author Lewis Carroll. It is believed to have inspired the chess game in *Through the Looking Glass*.

Sedges, reeds and teazles can be seen on the river bank and the air of the moor is filled with birdsong. The moor is known to botanists for its many interesting plants, including several species of orchids.

scatter of modern houses, but this is soon followed by the first of the older buildings, the stone-built Plough Inn, with its slate roof. The little church is now only a portion of a once grander building, and the village school, next door, is now a private house, though it still has its school bell. There are reminders of a certain grandeur in the Manor Farm and the old Manor House. When moves to drain the moor

began in the 19th century, notices were posted in all the Otmoor towns, and everywhere they were pulled down and destroyed, except for Noke, where there were no protests.

Noke is very much a village of farmhouses and cottages, well spaced down the lane. Look out on the right-hand side for Vine Cottage, with its thatched roof topped by a thatch pheasant, and across the

Near Oddington, the river appears as the New River Ray, a straight cutting that now carries the main flow of water from the moor. Bounded by trees and popular with swans, it is attractive, but nothing can disguise its artificial character. The flow is monitored: there is a monitoring station by the bridge at Stage 7, where a post shows the

▶ This small church was once part of a grander building in the village of Noke, which lies on the edges of Otmoor.

height of flood waters and levels are controlled by sluices.

The walk now leaves the moor at the village of Oddington **D**. There was once an abbey here, but as early as the 12th century there were

ALL PHOTOS CHRIS ANDREWS

The History of Otmoor

Otmoor is an area of low-lying land. The rising ground that surrounds it has been settled for centuries and contains the seven Otmoor towns, as they are always known, though none is more than a village. Centuries ago it was a wasteland, an area of swamp and bog, inadequately drained by the River Ray. The Romans came and with typical persistence constructed a road through the heart of the moor, but otherwise man did little to change the area. It remained waterlogged, a huge bog resting on a 450-foot (137-metre) deep layer of clay. It was, however, greatly valued by the inhabitants of the Otmoor towns. In winter, when it became a shallow lake, geese made their home here and were a much-prized source of food; in summer sheep grazed, though they were prone to foot-rot; and the sedges and reeds were useful for thatching. The Normans established a Moor Court at Beckley to control and look after the rights of the common. All that changed at the beginning of the 19th century.

It began in 1801 when the Duke of Marlborough applied for permission to drain part of the moor. In 1815 Parliament approved the enclosure of Otmoor. It allowed the village poor to have a share in the drained land — provided they paid their share of the drainage work and met the cost of erecting fences and hedges. As this was far beyond their means, they lost all rights to the common.

The work began, but met with violent opposition. Embankments for drainage ditches were broken in almost as soon as they were built and fences pulled down. The Otmoor riots lasted into the 1830s and the authorities could do little to prevent them. In September 1830 a number of Otmoor men were arrested and carted off to Oxford for trial, but it was the time of the great fair in St Giles and in the confusion every prisoner escaped.

In time, however, peace returned and the moor was developed into the landscape we see today. The winding, sluggish River Ray was given a new straight, fast-flowing channel and was fed by a series of drainage ditches. The moor was divided into a pattern of square fields.

complaints that the area was 'more suitable for an ark' and it was abandoned. The church still has an imposing square 13th-century tower with lancet windows.

FARMLAND

The remainder of the walk is now on minor roads back to Islip **A**. The route passes Logg Farm, with its imposing avenue of trees and its gallops and fences for steeplechase training. This is peaceful farming land, divided up by little streams. On the right, just beyond the small bridge at the edge of Islip, is a field of bumps and hollows, site of an old moated house. The final section through the village itself passes attractive cottages and the old almshouses of Tompkins Terrace before returning to the start.

▼ The bridleway runs near to the drainage ditch that controls the water level of this once marshy area.

The uninhabited expanse of Otmoor is rich in birdlife. It is a favourite stopping-off place for migrating birds and has its own attractive array of residents. Varied bird song can be heard — the skylark and meadow pipit and, lower down the scale, the wood pigeon and partridge.

STANTON HARCOURT

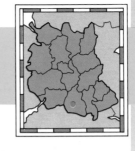

DEREK PRATT. INSET: P. HEARD/FRANK LANE PICTURE AGENCY

FACT FILE

🚶 Stanton Harcourt

🗺 Pathfinder 1116 (SP 40/50), grid reference SP 416056

miles 0 1 2 3 4 5 6 7 8 9 10 miles
kms 0 1 2 3 4 5 6 7 8 9 10 11 12 13 14 15 kms

◔ Allow 2 hours

▬ Easy; flat tracks and meadow paths that require waterproof shoes after rain

P At the Harcourt Arms

🏨 The Harcourt Arms

---

surviving Early English rood screens — it dates from the 13th century — and the standard that was borne by Sir Robert Harcourt at the Battle of Bosworth in 1485.

POETIC EPITAPH

On the south exterior wall of the church there is an epitaph to John Hewet (aged 25) and Sarah Drew (aged 18), who were killed by lightning while in a haycock on 31st July 1718. The epitaph was written by the poet Alexander Pope, who was staying at the manor in Stanton Harcourt, completing the fifth volume of his translation of *The Iliad*.

Just to the south of the village, on

◄*The River Thames winds its way through water meadows in this predominantly flat countryside. Snake's head fritillary (inset), found in the area, is now a rare wet meadow plant. This idyllic country cottage (below) is in the village of Sutton.*

From an ancient village, across meadowland to the River Thames

The River Thames near Stanton Harcourt, west of Oxford, has a different character to the fashionable river of regattas and straw boaters commonly associated with the area. Here it passes through remote countryside of lush water meadows. Good tracks connect these meadows with the village.

The village is dominated by the buildings of the Manor House that belonged to the Harcourt family from the 12th to the 18th centuries. The church of St Michael **Ⓐ** is situated close to the Manor House and contains a fine collection of monuments of all periods. Also inside the church is one of the oldest

DEREK PRATT

THE WALK

STANTON HARCOURT

The walk starts from the parish church of St Michael **Ⓐ** *at Stanton Harcourt. This is tucked away from the road opposite the Harcourt Arms, which has a car park.*

1 Return to the road and go right, passing the Harcourt Arms on your left. Follow the pavement until the road bends left.

2 Turn right along a rough lane signposted as a public footpath. Pass a school on your right and fork left to follow the metalled, tree-lined path. Pass an adventure playground on your left, cross a footbridge and reach a road.

3 Turn right along the road, ignore the footpath to the left at a bend and the junction and follow the road's continuation as a signposted path to the Thames. As you approach the far end of the field, veer right to a gate.

4 Do not follow the track ahead; instead, be careful to veer left to a footbridge in the far left corner of the next field. Cross the bridge.

5 Turn right along a track. Cross a footbridge beside a flat bridge ahead. Maintain your direction at a crosstrack immediately on the far side of the bridge, walking with a fence on your right. Take a footbridge to the left of a gate in the next corner and go ahead with a fence still on your right.

6 Turn right over a waymarked stile in the corner, go ahead 20 yards (18 metres) and turn left over a footbridge. Continue over a stile in the fence on the far side of the hedge. Go straight ahead across a meadow to the river.

7 Turn right along the Thames Path **Ⓑ**. This bears away from the river as it curves left. Reach the far right-hand corner of the meadow.

8 Go through the waymarked gate, cross a small enclosure surrounded by trees, ignoring a gate on your left, to another waymarked gate preceded by a concrete bridge. Take this and bear left to cross the field diagonally.

9 Ignore a gate on your right in the corner, but go ahead through a waymarked gate to follow a hedge on your right.

10 Turn right over a stile beside a gate into a metalled, hedged lane. The Thames Path turns left along a bridleway, but the lane goes straight ahead to the road in Stanton Harcourt.

11 Turn right for Manor House **Ⓒ** and church.

---

the site of a World War II airfield, stood the stones that gave Stanton its name. Such sacred prehistoric sites are believed by some to be guarded by 'spirits'. When these stones were disturbed by the construction of the airfield in 1940, a German fighting plane just happened to appear to strafe the workmen with bullets — although no one was killed by the gunfire.

The Thames Path **Ⓑ** is joined at Skinner's Weir, where there used to be a footbridge across the river. This is part of the 175-mile (280-km) walking route from the Thames Barrier to the river's source, which has become a National Trail.

HARCOURT MANOR

Much of the Manor House **Ⓒ** was demolished when the First Earl of Harcourt moved to Nuneham Courtenay in the 18th century. However, the tower, known as Pope's tower (where Alexander Pope worked for two years on his translation of Homer's *Iliad*) still stands. Also remaining is the Great Kitchen, which is one of the most important and complete medieval kitchens in England. There is also a gate house and a formal garden.

◄*The tower of Harcourt Manor, built in the 15th century by the Harcourt family. This tower is known as Pope's tower, as the poet spent two years here translating Homer's* Iliad, *completing it in 1718. The medieval kitchen, church, chapel and parsonage are still standing.*

DEREK PRATT

An ancient image and a country house, both carved in chalk

▲ *Ashdown House, given to the National Trust in a near-derelict state in 1956, has been well restored. The burnet companion moth (inset) flies by day in summer, like the burnet moths.*

On the downs above the Vale of the White Horse, ranged along the Ridgeway, there is a collection of ancient sites. This walk visits some of these and heads across rolling, empty downland to an exquisite, little-known country house. Whitehorse Hill, where the walk starts, is the highest point on the downs. The White Horse ❶, 376 feet (115 m) long, that is cut into its slopes is best seen from below; close to, it loses all definition (see box on page 88). In order to preserve it for future generations, visitors are requested not to walk on the horse.

DRAGON HILL

The viewpoint just above the horse commands a great sweep of the vale and provides the best view of The Manger, a dry valley cut into the scarp slope, and Dragon Hill ❷, a flat-topped mound where St George supposedly slew a dragon. The spot where the creature's blood is said to have spilled out is marked by a bare patch where nothing ever grows.

On the crest of the hill is Uffington Castle ❸, normally classed as an Iron Age hill fort. It commands a fine 360 degree view, but, even allowing for the effects of time on the ramparts and ditch, makes an unconvincing fort. This enclosure may have been used in the Iron Age, but it probably predates the period and may be a religious rather than a defensive site.

A gate takes you onto the Ridgeway ❹, which can lay claim to being the oldest pathway still in use in the world; in ancient times, the relatively dry ridge of the downs would have made for much easier going than the damp, heavily wooded low ground to the east. It is now part of the Ridgeway Path, a long-distance route that includes part of another ancient trackway, the Icknield Way, and runs for 85 miles (137km) from Buckinghamshire to Wiltshire.

The route turns off towards the heart of the Lambourn Downs and a landscape of huge, rolling fields, their contours traced by tractor trails through the crops or by the furrows of the plough. Some of the hills are marked by the gallops of the local racing stables. This is empty country, with hardly a building to be seen apart from seemingly abandoned barns. As you walk between the fields, you may put up a partridge or startle a lapwing into flight.

The route climbs Weathercock Hill. There used to be a racetrack on this windy height; what looks to be a shrubby hump to the left of the path conceals the remains of the building where the lathered horses were rubbed down after a race.

FACT FILE

✳	Whitehorse Hill, 10 miles (16km) east of Swindon, off the B4507
▭	Pathfinder 1154 (SU 28/38), grid reference SU 297864

miles 0 1 2 3 4 5 6 7 8 9 10 miles
kms 0 1 2 3 4 5 6 7 8 9 10 11 12 13 14 15 kms

◗	Allow 5 hours
▬	Mostly on broad, rough tracks. Two short, fairly steep ascents. The descent from Weathercock Hill can be slippery and difficult at times. Good walking boots or shoes recommended.
P	National Trust car park at start. If full, there is another car park further downhill. Alternatively, park at Ashdown Park and begin the walk from stage 4
▦	None on the route; The Rose and Crown pub in Ashbury and the White Horse Inn at Woolstone
⌐⌐ I	Ashdown House (National Trust) open April–Oct, Wed and Sat, 2–6pm; guided tours only (free for NT members). Ashdown Park and Weathercock Hill (National Trust) open all year Sat–Thurs dawn–dusk, admission free

THE WALK

WHITEHORSE HILL – ASHDOWN HOUSE

The walk begins in the car park on Dragonhill Road off the B4507.

1 Follow the path to the left of the hill fort to the viewpoint above the White Horse **A** and Dragon Hill **B**. Retrace your steps for just over 100 yards (90m). Turn left uphill, to the left of two thorn trees, to the trig point on the ramparts of Uffington Castle **C**. Continue ahead across the pasture to a gate and stile.

2 Go through and turn right onto the Ridgeway **D**. At the bottom of the hill, turn left on a crossing track. Continue ahead for 1½ miles (2.4km), rising gently then dropping to go through a line of trees. Bear slightly right to pass a small plantation on your left. Soon after the trees end, follow the track right.

3 Where the track bends left round a field, go straight on, uphill along a signposted bridleway. At the crest, by a large stone, go ahead and slightly right over the field as indicated by a footpath signpost. There is no clear path; aim just left of the pair of trees on the near horizon. Soon, a weather-cock **E** is visible between the trees. Cross the stile. This is open-access downland and there is no clear path ahead. Make for the weathercock, with Ashdown House **G** visible in the valley below.

Head downhill and slightly left to a stile opposite a T-junction. Take care; this steep slope, full of rabbit holes, can be slippery.

4 At the bottom of the hill, cross the stile and walk down the road opposite,

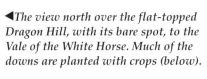

◀ *The view north over the flat-topped Dragon Hill, with its bare spot, to the Vale of the White Horse. Much of the downs are planted with crops (below).*

paintings, mostly portraits dating from the 17th century.

The route goes around the house, passing Ashdown Farm ❶, a lovely group of red-brick and stone buildings on your left. There is a view of Ashdown House down a once-proud avenue of limes. The trees were wrecked by gales in 1990 and have been cut back severely in an effort to save them.

As you go across the hill, the 17th-century weathercock ❸ from which its name derives, now ignominiously mounted on a telegraph pole, comes into view. Ashdown House ❻, built of chalk with Bath stone dressings, gleams in the sunshine. At dusk, a lamp is lit in the cupola, earning the house the nickname 'Lighthouse of the Downs'.

Like Weathercock Hill, the house now belongs to the National Trust. It was built in 1660 by Lord Craven; romantic legend suggests that he intended it for Queen Elizabeth of Bohemia as a refuge from plague-ridden London. However, she died in the capital in 1662.

It is more likely that the tall, four-square house, flanked by two detached pavilions, was a grand hunting lodge. The cupola and balustraded platform around it would have provided a fine place to view the hunt. The house now contains some of Lord Craven's

▶ *A thoroughbred horse – this is a racing area – stands by a lovely old brick and stone wall at Ashdown Farm.*

past Ashdown Farm ❶ and ahead through a waymarked metal gate. Bear right through a second metal gate, then immediately turn right through a third. Follow the field-edge path, signposted 'Ashbury', past an avenue, to Alfred's Castle ❽.

▶5 Just beyond the castle, turn right over a stile and walk along the field edge, with trees on your right, to a gate into woods. (If the gate is closed, bear left at the stile along a broad path through fields to the end of the woods. Bear right, round the trees, to pick up the route at stage 6.) Go through the gate and continue ahead through the trees to a broad, grassy ride. Turn left and follow this to its end.

▶6 Climb the log stile and turn right. Follow the green lane as it bears right around the trees, then turn left along the field edge to the road at Honeybunch Corner. Cross and follow the lane ahead, with trees to your right. Where the muddy track bends right, near the end of the field on your left, go straight on up the hill to a crossing track.

▶7 Turn left and continue straight ahead. Pass a barn on your left and go through a line of trees to the Ridgeway. Turn right, passing Waylands Smithy ❿ on your left after just over 300 yards (270m). Continue for a further 1 mile (1.6km) to a crossing track just before Whitehorse Hill.

▶8 Turn left down the track, then right along Dragonhill Road to return to the car park, and the starting point of the walk.

On your left, you pass Alfred's Castle ❽, a prehistoric site that was much depleted when the sarsen stones fortifying its ramparts were removed to be incorporated into the fabric of Ashdown House.

HERD OF DEER

The route then goes into Ashdown Park, the remains of the woodland that once surrounded the house. Here, you may see foxes, squirrels and a host of birds. Fallow deer also live in the mature, broadleaved woods, though they mostly keep to a private section south of the house. When the park is closed, the route skirts its edge.

A broad grassy swathe — one of four avenues that radiated from the house along the compass points — leads out onto the downland again. Wide tracks lined with beech and birch trees and bushes of thorn and dog rose take the route through huge arable fields back to the Ridgeway, and another impressive ancient site, Wayland's Smithy ❾. This is a Stone Age long barrow, shaded by a stand of beech trees and fronted by tall standing stones.

The passage tomb, now sealed, was built around 3330BC on the site of an even earlier wooden burial chamber. It was excavated in 1920; any burial goods had been plundered long before, but it still held the remains of at least eight people. The Saxons named it after Wayland the Smith, a legendary wizard who forged armour for the gods. According to legend, whoever left a horse overnight, and a coin on the stones, would find the animal shod in the morning.

The route back to Whitehorse Hill follows the Ridgeway. For much of the way, it is lined with flowers and bordered by mature hedges that are haunted by finches and butterflies.

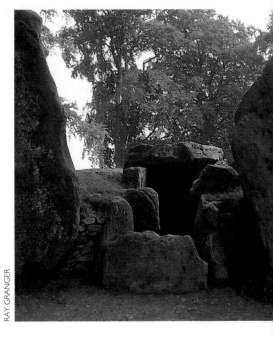

RAY GRANGER

▲ *Wayland Smithy on the Ridgeway is an impressive Stone Age long barrow, completed over 5,000 years ago.*

COMSTOCK PHOTOFILE LTD.

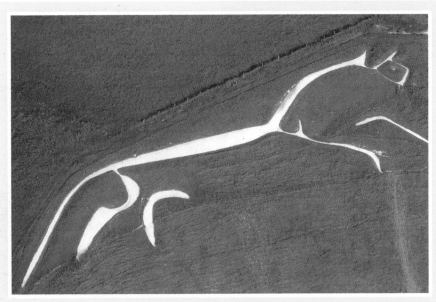

The Horse and the Dragon

Uffington's White Horse conceals many mysteries. No-one is sure of its age or purpose; there is even some doubt as to whether it represents a horse at all. It is most often dated at around 100BC, largely because a similar design appears on coins of that period. Many believe it to be older, however, arguing that the coins prove only that the symbol was recognizable and important at that period, not that it originated then.

The figure supposedly represents a Celtic god or a tribal symbol, and has historically been the centre of local festivals and customs. The most important was the 'scouring', when the image was cleaned and its lines newly cut. This took place every seven years or so at Whitsun, and was the occasion of a great fair within and around the castle. The festivities included games, dancing, drinking, singing and feasting. In 1780, the event attracted 30,000 people. The last scouring took place in 1857.

The Uffington White Horse is the oldest white horse in Britain and the only prehistoric one to survive unaltered.

The Manger, just below, has been associated with cheese-rolling, which is linked to sun worship, while legends of fertility cluster round the horse itself. For example, one story maintains that a maiden who spins three times in its eye at the correct time will see her future husband.

Believers in 'earth mysteries' point out the proximity of Whitehorse Hill to Dragon Hill, and that the figure resembles a dragon as much as it does a horse. In the Middle Ages, locals believed that it depicted St George's dragon. Dragons are traditionally a symbol of the power supposed to flow through ley lines. St Michael and St George, Christian dragon-slayers, are often associated with ancient pagan sites; either by legend as at Dragon Hill, or by having churches dedicated to them on hilltops and in henges.

One original theory has it that it was (or is) a message for extra-terrestrials — the figure is hard to make out when you are close to it, and, because of the angle of the slope, it is unclear from the valley; thus it must have been intended that it should be seen from the air.

ROLLRIGHT RAMBLES

29

FACT FILE

Salford, 14 miles (22.4km) south-west of Banbury, just off the A44

Pathfinders 1068 (SP22/32) and 1044 (SP 23/33), grid reference SP 286280

miles 0 1 2 3 4 5 6 7 8 9 10 miles
kms 0 1 2 3 4 5 6 7 8 9 10 11 12 13 14 15 kms

Allow 3½ hours

Two short, moderately steep ascents. Surfaced roads, rough tracks and paths on arable land that may be muddy, ploughed or overgrown at times

P Space for a few cars outside the church at the start

The Black Horse in Salford

Standing stones and a charming hamlet in the north Cotswolds

Salford is so named because it was on one of the old Cotswold salt routes. The precious mineral was brought down the Severn Valley, then taken across the wolds by pack-horses on its way to the Thames Valley and London.

The village's church **Ⓐ**, where this walk begins, was heavily restored by the Victorian, G E Street. A relief of a centaur over the south door is the main survival from the medieval church. The route goes through the churchyard, where fig trees hang over the wall, and skirts the edge of the village before heading out across the open countryside.

This part of the walk follows field paths through rich arable land. Many of the hedgerows have been grubbed out, and growing crops can make the paths difficult to follow. You climb a long field, where hares may sometimes be seen, to Brighthill Farm, then join a road that forms the boundary between Oxfordshire and Warwickshire. Its ridgetop position suggests that it is an ancient route; this is confirmed by the presence of the Rollright Stones.

The Whispering Knights **Ⓑ** stand in a conspiratorial huddle behind some railings in a field. Further on is the King Stone **Ⓒ**, an imposing monolith on a rise that commands wonderful views north over Long Compton into Warwickshire.

On the other side of the road is a henge of low stones, the Kings Men **Ⓓ**. It is supposedly impossible to count the stones and get the same result twice, though most people arrive at a number close to 76.

ROLLING STONES

The site has inspired many legends, including one that the stones roll downhill at certain times to take a drink from the river. They are supposedly the remains of an invading army, petrified by a witch; the Whispering Knights had lagged behind, plotting against their ruler.

You follow the old route, the Jurassic Way, to a crossroads, then turn down a quiet lane. A short way down to the right is Little Rollright **Ⓔ**, known in the *Domesday Book* as 'Rollandri'. There was a substantial village here, owned by Eynsham Abbey. By 1279, it had a population of 100 and a small monastery.

The village was swept away in the 16th century to make sheep pastures; 200 acres (80 hectares) were enclosed in 1517. An old moat,

▼*The Whispering Knights, the exposed remains of a burial chamber, look eerily human at times. Little Rollright (above left) has some charming old stone buildings, on which wall moss (seen inset with droplets of dew) grows.*

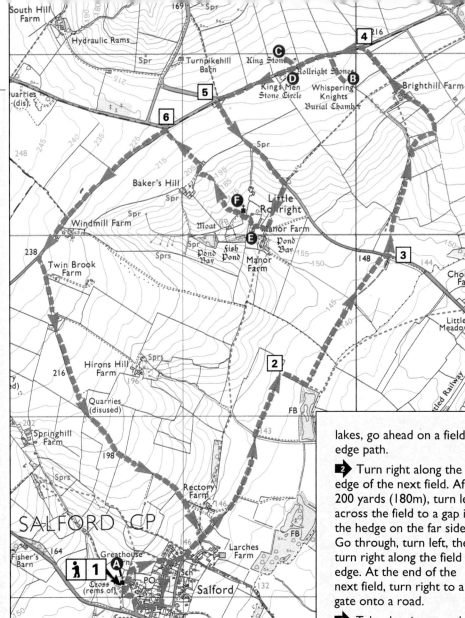

field, turn left along the field edge to see the Whispering Knights **B**. Return to the road and continue. Over a stile to the right, nearly 300 yards (270m) ahead, is the King Stone **C**; the Kings Men **D** are a little further on, to your left. Continue ahead to a crossroads.

5 Turn left. After a little over 600 yards (540m), turn right on a path marked 'William d'Arcy Dalton Way'. Go straight ahead down the hill into Little Rollright **E**. At the bottom of the field, turn right. Follow the winding lane past the manor and the rectory to the church **F**. Beyond the churchyard, a footpath leads uphill to the right. Aim just left of the barns at the top. Go through the gap and follow a stony track, ahead and a little right, to a road.

6 Turn left. After ⅝ mile (1km), shortly beyond a pair of isolated houses, turn left on a tarmac road marked 'Unsuitable for motors'. This becomes a rough track between walled fields. Follow it to a T-junction by Larches Farm. Turn right. At the end of the drive, turn right and follow the road into Salford. Bear right at the end, and continue following the road round to the right to return to the church.

lakes, go ahead on a field-edge path.

2 Turn right along the edge of the next field. After 200 yards (180m), turn left across the field to a gap in the hedge on the far side. Go through, turn left, then turn right along the field edge. At the end of the next field, turn right to a gate onto a road.

3 Take the signposted footpath opposite, across a field. Go through the hedge at the wooden signpost and follow the left-hand field edge. Bend right, to the top of the hill. Go left over a stile and across two pastures. Continue to the right of the farm buildings, then ahead up the farm drive to a road.

4 Turn left. At the next

SALFORD – LITTLE ROLLRIGHT

The walk starts at the parish church **A** *in Salford.*

1 Walk to the right of the church. Follow a stone wall on your right to a kissing-gate. Go diagonally right across the field and

through the gap in the far corner. Bear right over a stile onto a side-road. Turn left at the end, then first left up a drive marked 'Larches Farm'. Continue ahead on a broad track past Rectory Farm. Where this ends, by a right turn signposted to the trout

RAY GRANGER

monastic fish ponds and a few earth-works are all that remains of the old village.

Today, Little Rollright consists of a farm, the stone-built Manor (1633), the Old Rectory (1640) and the Church of St Philip **F**, which has a pleasing rustic simplicity. In the chancel, which was built by the

◀ *The Old Rectory's roof has buckled slightly under the weight of its slates.*

monks, are two fine, large, 17th-century wall tombs.

You climb back through fields to the ridgetop road, then turn off on an old packhorse route to Chipping Norton, which takes you to the north end of Salford. The last section of the walk winds through the village. It has no particularly fine buildings, but there are plenty of charming cottages, and an abundance of fragrantly flowery gardens.

30

BUCKINGHAMSHIRE

local napped flint and brick architecture, Holmer Green is reached over flat upland fields.

Holmer Green has grown in the last two decades from a sleepy little hilltop village to a large urban spread of housing estates, but the core of the village, its duckpond **C**, its common and pubs, are still intact. The charming duckpond is tended, planted and stocked with fish and fat, cheerful ducks by the Holmer Green 'Pond Committee'.

The flinty sunken lane winding

◀ *The charming duckpond at Holmer Green. (inset) The singing skylark nests on the ground. (below) St John the Baptist Church at Little Missenden.*

Through water meadows and along old footpaths

This attractive walk between the two villages of Little Missenden and Holmer Green offers a variety of splendid scenery. The route starts from the riverside then goes uphill to Holmer Green, along ancient sunken lanes and field paths with spectacular views before returning downhill to Little Missenden.

The walk starts on a broad track alongside the River Misbourne which tumbles over a clean gravel bed and is edged by ragged, bright green weed. Water meadows meet the steep, tree-fringed hills. The path leads over fields, across a farm track and crosses the edge of the lakes **A** below Shardeloes **B**, an impressive house standing high on the hill. The lakes were landscaped by Humphrey Repton in the late 18th century. Today they are home to a great variety of water birds: moorhens, coots and many types of duck, and provide a delightful approach to the cricket field.

Shardeloes, which overlooks the lakes, was built by Stiff Leadbetter in 1766 and, later, much altered by Robert Adam. It is a majestic, square, white-stuccoed house. Its large north-facing portico

was designed by Adam and James Wyatt. It was the home of a prosperous local merchant until after World War II when it was sold and converted into flats and maisonettes.

From Shardeloes' drive there are spectacular views over the valley to the hills which shelter the town of Old Amersham. In the spring blue-

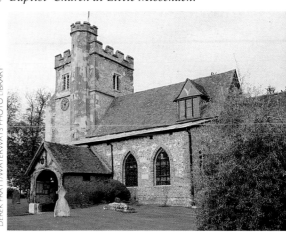

FACT FILE

✳ Little Missenden, Bucks

▭ Pathfinder 1138 (SU 89/99), grid reference SU 927990

miles 0   1   2   3   4   5   6   7   8   9   10 miles
kms 0   1   2   3   4   5   6   7   8   9   10   11   12   13   14   15 kms

◐ Allow 2 hours

▭ Some hills, tracks and footpaths. Walking shoes recommended after rain

P Roadside, in Little Missenden near The Red Lion pub

▭ The Red Lion pub at Little Missenden. The Earl Howe and The Bat & Ball at Holmer Green

bells garland the path into the valley past Wheatley Wood with hills rising steeply on each side.

Passing through the hamlets of Mop End and Beaumont End, both of which have fine examples of the

downhill from Holmer Green to Little Missenden has joined these two communities for over a thousand years. The ancient hedges and the presence of the plant dog's mercury in Coleman's Wood give proof of the antiquity of the lane.

From Little Missenden it is well worth a short diversion from the walk to see the Saxon church of St John the Baptist **D**, which lies just to the left of the Manor House, almost in its garden. The unmoulded arches of the church are 12th century and the 13th-century chancel has a three-lancet east window. A 20th-century addition is the new vestry with a steeply-hipped roof. Inside there are some 12th- and 13th-century wall paintings; the best preserved shows St Christopher with the infant Jesus at his feet.

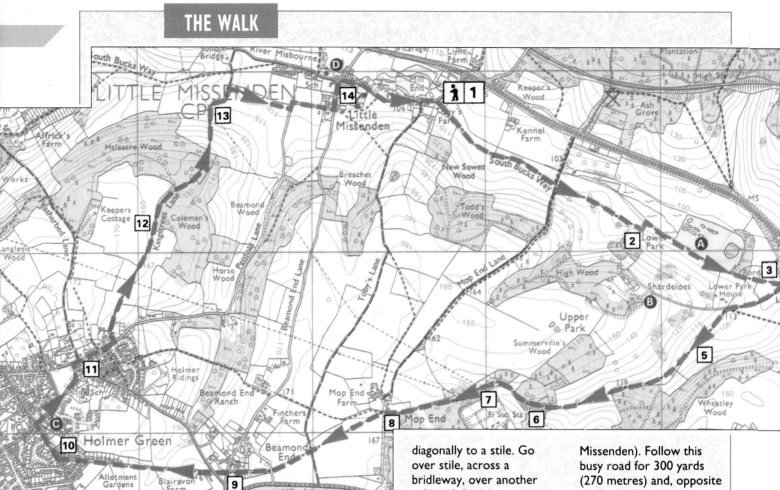

LITTLE MISSENDEN–HOLMER GREEN

The walk begins from The Red Lion pub at Little Missenden.

1 From The Red Lion pub walk along road and where it bends left, cross and go through a gate and follow a wide track ahead for 1½ miles (2.4 km). The River Misbourne is across the fields to the left. Ignore side turnings and at a junction of paths, continue ahead through a gate and along a grassy track. By a large clump of trees bear slightly left to a double stile ahead.

2 Go over a stile and bear left towards the lakes **A** and keep along fence to a stile. Go over the stile and continue in next field to a gate.

3 Go through a gate into the cricket field and cross it, passing the pavilion to a gate on the far side.

4 Turn sharp right and follow the drive to Shardeloes **B** for ¼ mile (400 metres). Opposite a large white house, take second path through a gate on the left.

5 Follow this path with a hedge/fence on the left, straight ahead along the valley ignoring all side turnings to woodland.

6 At the wood, cross a stile and ignoring another stile on the left which only gives access to a wooden 'hide', turn right uphill for a few yards and then bear left along a clear path.

7 The path continues uphill, soon emerging into a small grassy open area. Continue ahead crossing a grassy track on the left. Follow this fenced path along the edge of woodland, passing a large pylon, and bear right along a clear path, soon passing a house and on to the lane at Mop End.

8 Cross the lane to a stile and go over field diagonally to a stile. Go over stile, across a bridleway, over another stile and then across another field to a stile by Finchers Lodge. Go down a fenced path to right of Finchers Lodge to emerge on a lane among a group of flint cottages. Continue to end of lane.

9 Cross road and go down path in front of you by the 'White House'. At the end cross road to another path. Go through farm gate and bear right round farm buildings and follow path alongside hedge to Holmer Green. At stile go straight up Hogg Lane to main road – Earl Howe Road.

10 Turn right along Earl Howe Road, soon passing the Earl Howe pub. At crossroads by Holmer Green duckpond **C** turn right along pond approach. After 200 yards (180 metres), cross the village common past the children's play area to the Bat & Ball pub.

11 Go past the pub and turn right along Penfold Lane (signposted to Little Missenden). Follow this busy road for 300 yards (270 metres) and, opposite Winters Way, go down a bridleway by Holmer Green Farm. (This path is muddy in wet weather.)

12 Follow this wide path downhill, then uphill between hedges for 1½ miles (2.4 km). After ½ mile (800 metres) the path enters woodland. Continue, ignoring all side turnings and keeping to the clear track through the woods. After 1 mile (1.6 km) the path emerges from the woods and goes downhill between high hedges.

13 After about 1½ miles (2.4 km) from Holmer Green, look out for a stile/gate on the right. Go through and across a large field to a gateway. Here, turn left along Penfold Lane to reach Little Missenden.

14 At the crossroads, turn left to see the Church of St John the Baptist **D**. Then return to the crossroads by the Manor House and go past the Red Lion pub to where the car is parked.

THE HELLFIRE WALK

BUCKINGHAMSHIRE

Through beautiful countryside in an area with a colourful past

Mention West Wycombe to anyone and the subject of the Hellfire Caves will sooner or later come up. The Dashwood family who bought the estate in 1698 were a colourful lot and none more so than Sir Francis, the second baronet, who inherited in 1724. In the 1740s, he founded the notorious Hellfire Club, also known punningly as the 'Knights of St Francis of Wycombe'. This was a dining club with a difference and the members definitely did not take monastic vows of chastity. It existed for lively

conversation, dining and womanizing and the 'monks' included the painter William Hogarth, John Wilkes and other leading Whig politicians, as well as poets and members of the gentry.

The man-made Caves **B**, excavated in 1748–1750, tunnel into the hillside for ¼ mile (400 metres) with numerous side chambers and passages. These were used for great candlelit dinners, some probably for the Hellfire Club; however, the Club more usually met at Medmenham Abbey on the River Thames.

PICTURESQUE VILLAGE

The walk starts in the attractive village of West Wycombe **A**, which has many timber-framed buildings including the Church Rooms, originally built as eight medieval lock-up shops with a large hall above. There

The Mausoleum is a flint folly in the landscaped gardens of West Wycombe Park. The marbled white butterfly (inset) is found in grassy places in the area. Its caterpillars feed on grasses.

are also good Georgian brick houses and the view up Church Lane, with its narrow brick houses climbing the hill, is truly memorable. Both the village and the mansion in its park belong to the National Trust. The present Sir Francis Dashwood still lives in the house.

Leaving the village, the route climbs up to the Iron Age hillfort

FACT FILE

✳ West Wycombe in the north-west area of High Wycombe

▭ Pathfinder 1138 (SU 89/99), grid reference SU 825947

miles 0 1 2 3 4 5 6 7 8 9 10 miles
kms 0 1 2 3 4 5 6 7 8 9 10 11 12 13 14 15 kms

◔ Allow 2 ¼ hours

▬ Easy with some uphill walking

P West of West Wycombe Garden Centre at west end of village

T Buses run between High Wycombe and West Wycombe

▦ Public houses and shops in West Wycombe High Street.
⑪ Gardener's Cottage in Garden Centre

WC At car park near Garden Centre

⌂ West Wycombe village and park are owned by the National Trust. The house and grounds are open from Sunday to Thursday, 2.00–6.00pm, in June, July and August. There is an admission charge. The privately owned West Wycombe Caves are closed at present while they are being refurbished.

G R RICHARDSON/NATIONAL TRUST PHOTOGRAPHIC LIBRARY. INSET: ROBIN FLETCHER/SWIFT PICTURE LIBRARY

THE WALK

WEST WYCOMBE

The walk begins on the west side of West Wycombe Centre at village Ⓐ.

1 From the car park next to the West Wycombe Garden Centre at the west end of the village, turn right to the main road, then left to walk down the High Street. Turn left through the archway in Church Rooms, the jettied, timber-framed building with a large clock on a bracket, and walk up Church Lane. Near the top, turn left and walk past the elaborate flintwork façade to the Caves Ⓑ. Immediately after this, leave the tarmac lane and turn right on to the path that climbs steeply uphill, soon turning right up steps to the brow. Here turn left on to a wide grass path up to the Mausoleum Ⓒ. Go right of this on to the path through the churchyard Ⓓ and into the Church of St Lawrence.

2 After visiting the church, leave the churchyard by the north gate and walk along the left edge of the car park towards white gates, which belong to Windyhaugh House. Take the track to the left of the house and follow it for 1 mile (1.6 km) through woods to Butler's Hangings Nature Reserve Ⓔ. Follow a fenced path to a road, go straight on across a field, a lane, another road and a pasture, until you reach a lane at Chorley Farm Ⓕ.

3 Go uphill to the left of the farmhouse on a metalled lane, signposted as a bridleway. Keep on the metalled lane, ignoring footpath junctions, until over the summit. Where the lane descends steeply turn left into Great Cockshoots Wood (indicated by an arrow painted on a beech tree). Go through the woods with white paint on trees and saplings to show the way, emerge over a stile damaged by a fallen tree and go diagonally right across the field to a stile. Go over the stile, descend through two fields with fine views of West Wycombe and the Park Ⓖ. Cross the stile in the corner of the field, and walk along the pavement alongside the A40 with a view towards the lake Ⓗ, passing the entrance gates Ⓙ to West Wycombe House Ⓚ. Return to the entrance gates and continue walking alongside the A40. At the junction turn left. Return to car park.

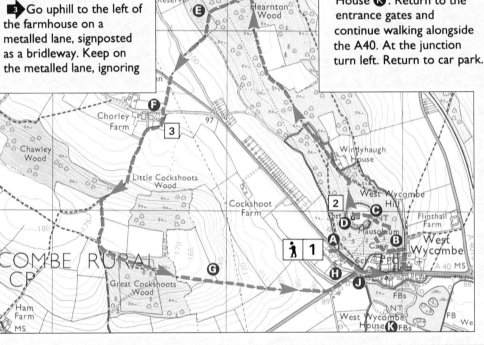

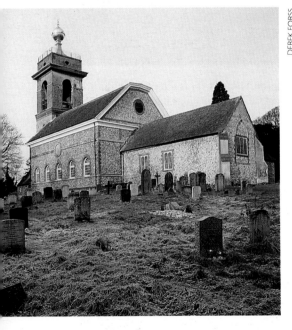

DEREK FORSS

where the 18th-century Sir Francis dramatically rebuilt most of the parish church Ⓓ in Georgian style, crowning the tower with a golden ball in which people could sit. Next to the church, on a site commanding superb views towards High Wycombe, Sir Francis built a hexagonal structure. This is the Mausoleum Ⓒ, designed in 1763 and intended for the ashes of members of The Hellfire Club.

From the church the route continues north along the beechwooded ridge with fine views to east and west before descending towards the nature reserve Ⓔ and the valley.

The grand 18th-century church of St Lawrence, crowned with a golden ball, dominates the village of West Wycombe.

Passing 17th-century timber-framed farmhouses and barns in the valley bottom Ⓕ, the route then climbs up the ridge and left into Great Cockshoot Woods. From there it descends the ridge with fine views over the village of West Wycombe and the Park Ⓖ towards the lake Ⓗ.

STATELY MANSION

On entering the village again, the route passes the entrance gates Ⓙ to West Wycombe House Ⓚ, transformed by Sir Francis Dashwood using the architects John Donovell and Nicholas Revett. The house is striking, with ochre-coloured render and cool stone. The park in the valley of the River Wye was gradually filled with buildings, many in the form of Greek or Roman temples.

Overlooking the Vale

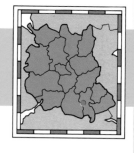

▲*Perched on Brill Common is a 17th-century post mill. Balanced on a central post, the whole mill can rotate to point into the wind. Marsh marigolds (left) grow by the nearby stream.*

From a hilltop village along quiet country lanes and fields

The walk begins at the edge of the attractive village of Brill. This is an area of common land, full of humps and hollows, the marks of old pits from which clay was dug for brick-making and a pottery industry that dates back to the Middle Ages. The village is 613 feet (187m) above sea level and looks out over the Vale of Aylesbury. The most prominent building is the 17th-century windmill **Ⓐ**. This is one of the oldest post mills in England. The actual milling machinery is in the weather-boarded 'buck' to which the sails are attached. This is balanced on a central post — hence the name 'post mill' — and the whole structure can be rotated to bring the sails into the wind.

The route leads through hills and fields to the hamlet of Boarstall. Once, there was a considerable village here, dominated by a fortified manor house surrounded by a moat. Much has gone, but a good deal of interest still remains.

MEDIEVAL MANOR HOUSE

The little church of St James was consecrated in 1418, but was largely rebuilt after the Civil War. It is quite a plain structure, but has a fine, wooden 17th-century pulpit. In the churchyard, an ornate gate, embellished with a hunting horn, emblem of the Aubrey family, provides a glimpse into the grounds of Boarstall Tower **Ⓑ**. The tower was originally the gatehouse to the now-demolished medieval manor house and it rose up, battlemented and severe, above the moat. Later, it was domesticized, and its Tudor and Jacobean windows give it a rather more homely look. It is now in the care of the National Trust.

The road passes a number of attractive farms. The older part of

▼*Boarstall Tower was built in the 14th century as the gatehouse to a long-since-demolished fortified mansion.*

FACT FILE

- ☀ Brill, 6 miles (10km) north-west of Thame

- Pathfinder 1093 (SP 61/71), grid reference SP 652141

  miles 0 1 2 3 4 5 6 7 8 9 10 miles
  kms 0 1 2 3 4 5 6 7 8 9 10 11 12 13 14 15 kms

- ◷ Allow 2 ½ to 3 hours

- ▬ Mostly easy going on good paths

- P Brill Common, North Hill, adjacent to Brill windmill

- T Buses from Bicester and Aylesbury

- ¶ Full range of facilities at Brill

THE WALK

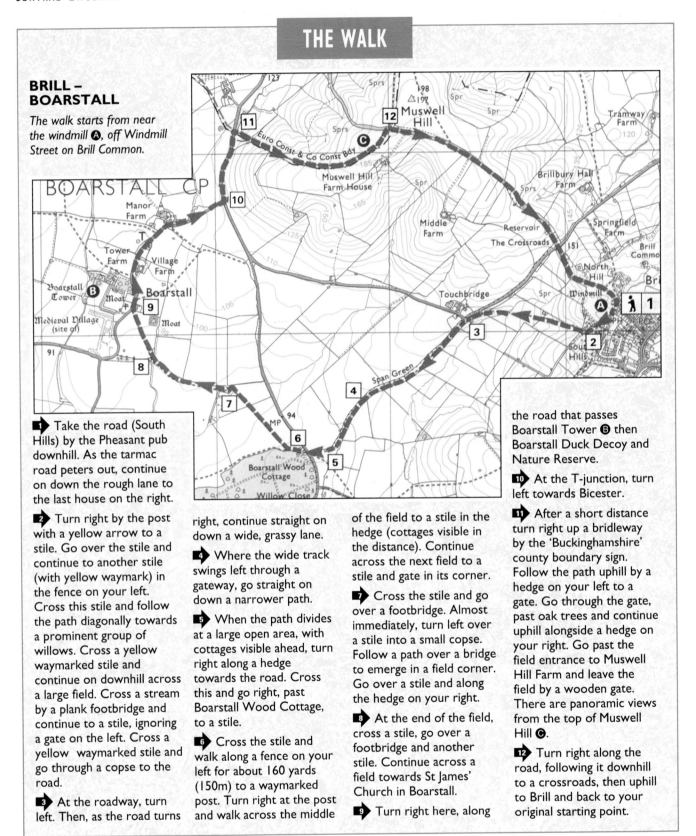

BRILL – BOARSTALL

The walk starts from near the windmill **A**, *off Windmill Street on Brill Common.*

1 Take the road (South Hills) by the Pheasant pub downhill. As the tarmac road peters out, continue on down the rough lane to the last house on the right.

2 Turn right by the post with a yellow arrow to a stile. Go over the stile and continue to another stile (with yellow waymark) in the fence on your left. Cross this stile and follow the path diagonally towards a prominent group of willows. Cross a yellow waymarked stile and continue on downhill across a large field. Cross a stream by a plank footbridge and continue to a stile, ignoring a gate on the left. Cross a yellow waymarked stile and go through a copse to the road.

3 At the roadway, turn left. Then, as the road turns

right, continue straight on down a wide, grassy lane.

4 Where the wide track swings left through a gateway, go straight on down a narrower path.

5 When the path divides at a large open area, with cottages visible ahead, turn right along a hedge towards the road. Cross this and go right, past Boarstall Wood Cottage, to a stile.

6 Cross the stile and walk along a fence on your left for about 160 yards (150m) to a waymarked post. Turn right at the post and walk across the middle

of the field to a stile in the hedge (cottages visible in the distance). Continue across the next field to a stile and gate in its corner.

7 Cross the stile and go over a footbridge. Almost immediately, turn left over a stile into a small copse. Follow a path over a bridge to emerge in a field corner. Go over a stile and along the hedge on your right.

8 At the end of the field, cross a stile, go over a footbridge and another stile. Continue across a field towards St James' Church in Boarstall.

9 Turn right here, along

the road that passes Boarstall Tower **B** then Boarstall Duck Decoy and Nature Reserve.

10 At the T-junction, turn left towards Bicester.

11 After a short distance turn right up a bridleway by the 'Buckinghamshire' county boundary sign. Follow the path uphill by a hedge on your left to a gate. Go through the gate, past oak trees and continue uphill alongside a hedge on your right. Go past the field entrance to Muswell Hill Farm and leave the field by a wooden gate. There are panoramic views from the top of Muswell Hill **C**.

12 Turn right along the road, following it downhill to a crossroads, then uphill to Brill and back to your original starting point.

Village Farm is dated 1737 and has little dormer windows set in a mossy, tiled roof, while the neighbouring Manor Farm is more imposing. Just beyond the farms is the entrance to the Boarstall Duck Decoy and Nature Reserve.

The road section of the walk ends at a path that climbs the rough grassy slope of Muswell Hill **C**, passing a group of old oak trees which are home to a family of green woodpeckers. From the top of the hill there is a panoramic view south

over the plain and north over more undulating farmland.

The final part of the walk is along a quiet country lane sheltered by hedgerows. The lane dips briefly down, before climbing back up the hill for the return to Brill.

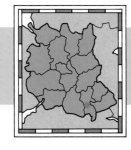
BUCKINGHAMSHIRE

PAUL FELIX. INSET: E.A.JANES/NATURE PHOTOGRAPHERS

▲ *Cottages with white-rendered witchert walls, often with thatched roofs, cluster around the village green at the southern end of Haddenham. The all-white Aylesbury ducks (left) used to be at the centre of the local economy.*

Picturesque villages around the valley of the River Thame

In the area to the west of Aylesbury are many charming villages containing rendered cottages, and gardens and lanes bounded by tile-coped walls. Many of the older buildings are in 'witchert', the local dialect name for cob or earth-wall construction (see box on page 100). These earth walls, often combined with sweeping, thatched roofs, lend great character to the villages.

The walk starts and finishes in the heart of the witchert country, Haddenham Ⓐ, a village almost a mile (1.6km) long, with three distinct focuses or 'ends'. The route passes through Townsend which has an attractive green surrounded by handsome witchert cottages, and Fort End, where five roads meet, but

begins at Church End, where the superb parish church and timber-framed Church Farmhouse overlook the village duckpond and green.

The church dates mainly from the 13th century, and has a particularly fine west tower. Inside, there is a plough carved on a bench end near the tower arch, and a carved monkey's face on the 15th-century wooden screen set in the tower arch.

WEALDEN HOUSE

Church Farmhouse is in the Kentish Wealden style, with projecting side wings and a recessed centre under a single roof. The church was once owned by Rochester Priory, so the 15th-century house may have been built by carpenters from Kent. Haddenham was a centre of the Aylesbury duck-rearing industry. Duck-keepers' cottages were built along Flint Street, which was originally called Duck Lane.

The route leaves Haddenham

THE WALK

HADDENHAM – CHEARSLEY – CUDDINGTON

The walk begins by St Mary's Church in Haddenham **Ⓐ**.

1 Walk down Flint Street to the west of the duckpond. At a T-junction, turn left onto Station Road. Beyond the railway, continue for about 500 yards (450m) to where the road bends slightly right.

2 Go left over a stile and ahead through two fields. Turn left. After about 220 yards (200m), turn right at a footpath sign across another field. Cross a main road and continue on a track. At the bottom of the valley, climb a stile and go half-left to a stile in the corner. Cross the iron bridge over the Thame.

3 Bear left between the river and the former millstream, then turn right to the bridge across the leat and race of Notley Mill **Ⓑ**. Over the bridge, turn right again. Go through a gate and follow the millstream. Beyond a dense hedge and a stile, turn left along a fenced path round the grounds of Notley Abbey **Ⓒ**. Go past some earthworks **Ⓓ** to Notley Farm.

4 Just beyond the farm entrance, climb a stile on your right and follow a track, with the dovecote **Ⓔ** off to your right. Go down to a stream and climb a stile. Head slightly left to a gap between a copse and a line of pollarded willows. Head for a stile to the left

of a stand of poplars. Cross, go over a footbridge and through Long Mead Copse ahead. Go over a stile and head uphill beside

a fence. Cross the railway line and continue ahead on a grassy track beside a hedge/fence. Cross a concrete farm road, and go

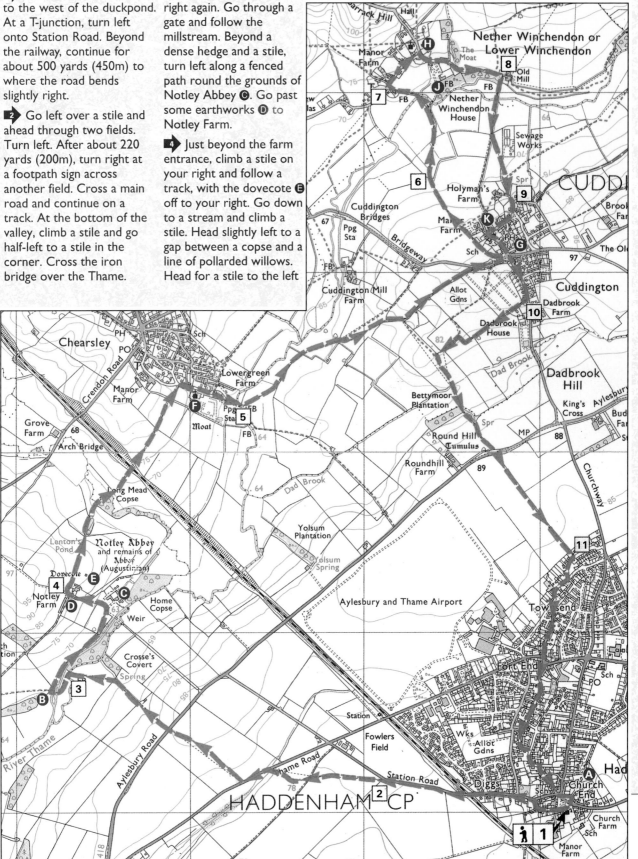

over a pasture and down to Church Lane. Turn right to Chearsley's church **F**. Continue ahead down the lane, which soon becomes a track.

5 Go through a kissing-gate and cross a footbridge over the Thame. Head diagonally left, then continue by a fence, roughly parallel to the river. Go over a stile, and head diagonally right across a field to climb the next stile. Bear diagonally right, to the right-hand one of two stiles. Walk up the track, to a road. Turn right along the far pavement into Cuddington. Just before you reach the green **G**, turn left onto a concrete road by The Lodge. Follow it to a cattle grid.

6 Continue over old water-meadows. Where the road turns right to a bridge, continue half-left ahead, and cross the river to a road.

7 Turn right to the church in Lower Winchendon **H**. Turn right again at the post box, onto a lane that passes the gates to Nether Winchendon House **J**. Continue walking along the lane to reach Winchendon Mill.

8 Turn right over a stile. Cross the River Thame on a footbridge and continue along a willow-lined ditch. Climb the left-hand stile and go diagonally left across a narrow field to a stile in the hedge. Cross a concrete road and

continue in the same direction to a stile in a fence. Bear half-right to another stile in the corner of the field, and cross this into a lane.

9 Turn left. At the end, turn right onto Lower Church Street, to pass Tyringham Hall **K**. Continue up Upper Church Street, go straight on over a crossroads and continue walking downhill for 300 yards (270m).

10 At a partly concealed footpath sign just before a thatched cottage, turn right. At the end of the track, climb a stile. Continue straight on for a short distance, then turn sharp left to follow a path through a field to a gate at the valley bottom. Climb

the stile by the gate. Keep straight on through a pasture and through a copse, then uphill alongside a hedge to the A418. Cross with care, then go straight ahead, keeping the hedge on your left.

11 Beside the garden walls of Cobwebs Cottage, cross a stile and turn right. Take the next right turn onto Rudd's Lane. At Townsend Green, head down a footpath in its far left corner. This emerges in Fern Lane, then Fort End. Walk down the High Street. At the King's Head, turn left onto a footpath. At the end turn right down The Croft, which winds into Gibson Lane. At the end, turn left back to Church End, and the start.

◄ *A timeless scene, with Aylesbury ducks loafing by Haddenham's pond. In the background is the 13th-century parish church and nearby is Church Farmhouse (above), probably built by Kentish carpenters. West of the village is the site of Notley Mill (below).*

across the railway line, which opened in 1906. In honour of the occasion, Baggs Lane was renamed Station Road. The station closed in the 1960s, but a new one was opened, further north, in 1987.

The route drops into the attractive valley of the Thame, lined with poplars, willows and alders, and crosses the river by Notley Mill **B**, a watermill that closed down in the 1920s. Its stream and leat remain, together with some walls, and a stretch of cobbles from its yard.

A path follows the tree-fringed mill leat towards Notley Abbey **C**, a community of Augustinian canons founded in the early 12th century by Walter Gifford. A few remnants of the church and cloister buildings have been incorporated in later barns. The sumptuous Prior's Lodgings, finished in 1530 shortly before the abbey was dissolved, survive as a house that later became famous as the home of Laurence Olivier and Vivien Leigh.

As you approach Notley Farm, a

ALL PHOTOS: PAUL FELIX

ALL PHOTOS: PAUL FELIX

◄ *There is a post box in an unusual stone pillar in front of Lower Winchendon's church, which is worth a visit for its interior. Back in Haddenham you can admire the delightful moulded brick chimneys of Cobwebs Cottage (right).*

modern stone farmhouse, you can see earthworks **D** associated with the medieval abbey farmstead. Among the farm buildings is a 15th-century cruck-built barn, which must have been the monastic tithe barn. To the east of the farm, the majestic abbey dovecote **E** stands isolated in an arable field.

On the other side of the railway is Chearsley, a village remarkable for its deep-cut lanes. St Nicholas's Parish Church **F** is very attractive and unpretentious, with white-washed walls, a Georgian west gallery and, unusually, two sets of Royal Arms. Immediately south of the church are the earthworks of a moated, medieval manor house that has long since been demolished.

Beyond, in Cuddington, there is a cut-off which allows you to miss out the loop to Lower Winchendon if you are pressed for time. The main route turns north at the edge of Cuddington's village green **G**, which still has its old parish pump and is surrounded by a delightful group of witchert cottages.

On the other side of the Thame you reach Lower Winchendon **H**. This small village has many timber-framed cottages and an excellent 16th-century manor farmhouse complete with barns. The atmospheric church interior boasts box pews, a three-decker pulpit, a squire's pew and a fine west gallery.

LINENFOLD PANELLING

Nether Winchendon House **J** has a medieval core, the best part of which is a room with Tudor linenfold panelling. The house was formerly owned by Notley Abbey, but owes much of its present appearance to Scrope Bernard, an amateur architect who 'gothicized' the building in around 1800.

You return through Cuddington, another village dominated by witchert walls and cottages, though Tyringham Hall **K** opposite the church is in stone. The hall is all that remains of a much larger Tudor mansion. Its gabled left wing was altered in 1609. Some of the mullioned, transomed windows are in stone, and some in rendered brick.

MOULDED CHIMNEYS

The route re-enters Haddenham near Cobwebs, a witchert cottage that is dwarfed by its ornate brick chimneys, which were added in the 1920s. As you meander through the village on the way back to the church, you pass many more cottages, walls and outbuildings in witchert. Even the Methodist chapel of 1822 in the High Street is built of this distinctive material.

Witchert Walls

Witchert is Buckinghamshire's version of the 'cob' of Devon and Dorset. The word is a corruption of 'white earth', which roughly describes the lime-rich subsoil. The material is found in medieval excavations, and its use continued until after World War I. Most villagers were proficient in its use, although bigger structures, particularly houses and barns, were almost always the responsibility of local professional builders.

To build a wall, heaps of subsoil were thoroughly wetted and mixed with chopped straw to make them workable. This mixture was laid in 'berries', each about 20 inches (50cm) high, on a stone rubble base, known locally as a 'grumpling'. As each layer dried, a further one was slapped on top until the required height was reached. The surface was then dressed smooth with a sharpened blade.

As you look at the boundary walls of a witchert construction, note the horizontal seams that delineate each berry, and the fragments of limestone and chopped straw visible in the walls. Witchert is a high quality cob, and successful walls need be only 9 inches (22cm) thick, compared with a Devon cob average of 20-30 inches (50-75cm).

Many witchert structures survive, although as no-one still practises the technique, the number is slowly diminishing as demolition and neglect slowly take their toll. However, the fact that so many buildings from the 17th, 18th and 19th centuries have survived demonstrates the durability of this material.

The structure of witchert is most easily seen in the tile-coped boundary walls.

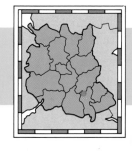

◀Following the die-straight line of a Roman road, Water Stratford Avenue crosses Oxford Water on a fine stone bridge. Beyond the rise, it continues between twin rows of lime trees (inset).

TOURAGE GILANSHAH. INSET: NATURE PHOTOGRAPHERS

Beside it is the Georgian Boycott Farm **C**, which has dormer windows with delightful hipped roofs.

Soon, you turn down another of Stowe's avenues. Water Stratford Avenue **D**, 1 mile (1.6 km) long, retains many of its 18th-century lime trees. It follows the course of the Roman road linking Winchester to Towcester and Watling Street. The line of the road continues into Stowe Park, and crosses the ornamental Oxford Water **E** by a superb stone bridge built in 1761.

The avenue leads up between the Boycott Pavilions of 1728, which acquired their French-style domes 30 years later. To the right of the avenue is the ha-ha that surrounded the original park in the 1720s. Beyond, largely screened by trees, are the buildings of Stowe School.

EQUESTRIAN STATUE

At the end of the double avenue you continue across the great north forecourt of Stowe House **F**. In the forecourt, though often hidden by cricket sightscreens, is a superb lead statue of a mounted George I, made by Van Nost in 1723 for £150.

The walk continues along the Roman road. On a rise to the left is a huge obelisk **G** which was erected in 1759 to commemorate General Wolfe's capture of Quebec.

▼The buildings of Stowe House were begun in 1676 by Sir Richard Temple.

Country lanes and formal avenues round a Classical garden

The centrepiece of this walk is the great 18th-century landscape garden of Stowe Park, described by James Thomson as 'The fair, majestic paradise of Stowe'. It was created between 1676, when Sir Richard Temple built a brick mansion here, and 1839, when the then owner, the 2nd Duke of Buckingham, became bankrupt.

Charles Bridgman, William Kent and Capability Brown landscaped the park, while leading architects such as Vanbrugh, Gibbs and Kent designed the 50 or more garden buildings. All are Classical in style, and include many temples. A public school was founded here in 1923, and the National Trust took over the gardens in 1989.

The walk begins in Chackmore **A**, whose main street has an appealing mix of buildings in limestone and brick. Just outside the village, you cross Stowe Avenue **B**, which runs for 1½ miles (2.4km) from lodges on the outskirts of Buckingham to a Corinthian arch erected in 1767.

The route follows a very straight country lane, laid out in 1773, when the area's open fields were enclosed.

FACT FILE

✶ Chackmore, 1½ miles (2.4km) north of Buckingham

▣ Pathfinder 1046 (SP 63/73), grid reference SP 684357

miles 0 1 2 3 4 5 6 7 8 9 10 miles
kms 0 1 2 3 4 5 6 7 8 9 10 11 12 13 14 15 kms

◑ Allow 2½ hours, plus at least 2 hours if visiting Stowe Landscape Gardens

▭ Mostly good walking on minor roads and well maintained paths through park and farmland. One or two brief ascents and descents

🅿 At the west end of Chackmore or on the village's main street

🆃 Buses to Buckingham, then a 1½ mile (2.4km) walk along Stowe Avenue

🍺 The Queen's Head pub in Chackmore

🍴 National Trust café in the grounds of Stowe House

🏰 Stowe House is sometimes open in school holidays (admission charge). For opening times and admission price of Stowe Landscape Gardens (National Trust), Tel. (01280) 822850

TOURAGE GILANSHAH

THE WALK

CHACKMORE — STOWE PARK

The walk begins by the Queen's Head pub in the village of Chackmore Ⓐ.

1 Follow the road west out of Chackmore, in the direction of Stowe. Cross Stowe Avenue Ⓑ. After about 100 yards (90m), go straight ahead onto an arrow-straight country lane. Follow this for a mile (1.6km) to a T-junction. Turn right and follow the road past Boycott Farm Ⓒ; and on to Water Stratford Avenue Ⓓ.

2 Turn right. At a crossroads, go straight on along the bridleway, passing through the gate screen to Stowe Park. Cross Oxford Water Ⓔ and continue straight ahead. The track passes across the forecourt of Stowe House Ⓕ, then the National Trust car park and the entry to the gardens. Wolfe's Obelisk Ⓖ is visible away to your left.

3 About 80 paces beyond the end of the park, turn right through a gate partly hidden by sycamore trees. The grassy track descends towards an avenue of red oak trees. Turn left onto this avenue, then right through a gate just before a copse. Follow the path alongside and then through the trees. Bourbon Tower Ⓗ is visible left as you come

out of the copse. Bear to the right of an obelisk Ⓙ on a low knoll. Stowe Castle Ⓚ is visible on the skyline. Go through a gate in the fence then down towards a tall lime at the edge of the park. Head for a lodge.

4 Go through the gate between the brick piers,

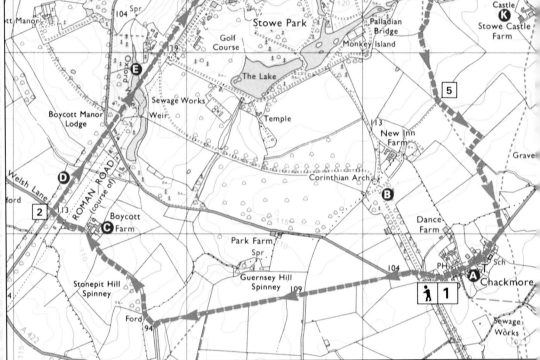

and down through pasture to a gate at the bottom of the valley. Go up a green lane, passing to the right of an ancient hollow oak. Follow the track across the field to its furthest corner.

5 Go through the hedge

and cross a track. Follow the hedge to your left down into the narrowest part of this long field. About halfway along the far end, to the left of some willow trees, is a way through the apparently

impenetrable hedge. Go through, climb a stile and head across a pasture to a stile right of a farmhouse. Continue across the next field to a road. Turn right and walk into Chackmore.

After leaving the Roman road you get a view along the Grecian Valley to the portico of the Temple of Concord and Victory. Beyond an avenue of red oaks that was planted in 1940, is the Bourbon Tower Ⓗ, which was built as a game-keeper's lodge in iron-rich Northamptonshire limestone and given an octagonal turret in 1845.

▶ *This fine, half-timbered cottage is in Chackmore, near the start.*

On the left, a granite obelisk Ⓙ, erected in 1864, commemorates the Royal Buckinghamshire Yeomanry Cavalry, a local militia regiment. Ahead, on the skyline, is what appears to be a medieval castle.

Stowe Castle Ⓚ is actually a remarkable eye-catcher built in the 18th century to be seen from Stowe. The battlemented U-plan building, which conceals a lean-to farmhouse, is visible for much of the way on the paths that return you to Chackmore.

From a peaceful Bedfordshire village to a mill in the surrounding fields

Nestling half way down a gentle valley of the River Great Ouse, the village of Stevington has a wealth of old and very attractive honey-coloured, stone buildings. These buildings were once used to promote crafts, including lacemaking and the weaving of mats from the riverside rushes. At the centre of the village is a fine 14th-century market cross **C** said to feature in John Bunyan's famous book *Pilgrim's Progress* as the place where Christian's burden fell from his shoulders.

THE HOLY WELL

Below the church of St Mary the Virgin **A** gushes a spring of water **B**, reputed never to run dry. This was a place of pilgrimage for people in the Middle Ages; the water was said to cure eye problems. The area is preserved by the Hunts and Beds Wildlife Trust because of the splendid growth of the wild flower butterbur. According to tradition, the large leaves of this plant were used for wrapping butter, which is how it got its English name.

FACT FILE

✳ Stevington, Bedfordshire, 4 miles (7 km) north-west of Bedford

⌨ Pathfinder 1001 (SP 85/95), grid reference SP 990536

miles 0   1   2   3   4   5   6   7   8   9   10 miles
kms 0   1   2   3   4   5   6   7   8   9   10   11   12   13   14   15   kms

◕ Allow 2 hours

▭ Easy walk mainly through fields. Not suitable for young children. Muddy in places. Walking shoes recommended

🅿 Near the Old Vicarage. (Continue straight over the crossroads by the village cross and turn into Church Lane which peters out at the church car park.)

🇹 Buses from Bedford to Odell stop at Stevington

🍴 Refreshments at Red Lion and Royal George pubs in Stevington

Inside the church of St Mary the Virgin are some remarkable 15th-century carvings of animals and men. Two men are lapping from bowls, while two are lounging in a drunken state. These carvings may be linked to church ale, maintained by a gift of 7 acres (3 hectares) of

▲ *A view of the restored 18th-century postmill in Stevington. (inset) The small heath butterfly is found in meadows, heaths and on roadsides.*
▼ *The 14th-century market cross was one of John Bunyan's preaching spots.*

land in the 15th century. Also inside the church is a marble memorial to Robert Taylor whose ancestors donated the carved figures on the nave's 15th-century oak roof. Two ruined chapels can be seen outside the church of St Mary the Virgin.

Beyond the church, in Court Lane, is another building with religious associations — the Baptist meeting house, built in 1720. An earlier meeting house had links with John Bunyan, the 17th-century

THE WALK

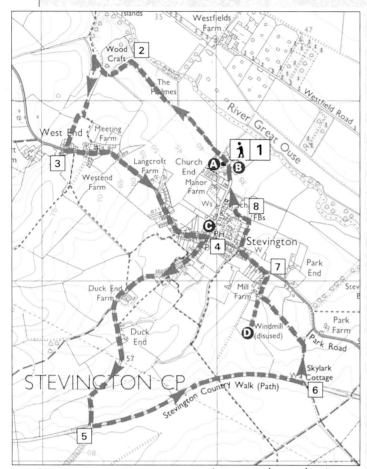

STEVINGTON

The walk begins from the church of St Mary the Virgin **A** *at Stevington.*

1 With the church wall on the left, walk ahead away from the village down a signposted footpath which passes the holy well **B** on the left. Go through a wooden kissing gate (arrow markers) into a meadow and walk ahead along a raised bank with the little river down on the right. Pass through a gateway in a hedge into another field (partly meadowland and scrub). Cross a stile (arrow marker) leading left into an arable field and turn right to continue ahead again with a wire fence on the right.

2 At the end of the field turn left and walk with the wire fence and a wood on the right. At the next corner cross a stile to the right, then one immediately to the left (markers on each) which leads on to a narrow fenced track. Cross a wooden footbridge into a rolling field. Turn immediately left along a ditch and hedgerow. At the end of the field, turn right past a metal field gate.

Bear left to some broken fencing at the entrance to an almost hidden track. Turn left and walk down the track which is closed in by trees, continuing ahead past a garage, right and between gardens to the road.

3 Turn left down the road (Court Lane) past the stone Baptist meeting house. In the centre of the village is the market cross **C** with the Red Lion pub nearby.

4 Turn right into Silver Street and walk past the Royal George pub and an assortment of stone cottages. Walk out of the village past the old stone buildings of Duck End Farm and continue along a narrow road to the old railway embankment.

5 Climb up and walk to the left along the top of the embankment. This is the path of the Stevington Country Walk. Walk past an old railway hut and then a cross path with stiles on either side of the track and continue on to fencing.

6 Turn left here through a gate and walk down a wide track to the left which winds through farmland. Before the path reaches the road, turn left along a wide signposted track which curves round the edge of the field towards some farm buildings. Just before these take the left-handed turn leading up to the windmill **D**. Return down the same track and carry on ahead past Windmill Cottage on the left to the road.

7 Turn left down the road. On the left is a Primitive Methodist Chapel, then a green. Shortly after this a footpath is signposted to the right. Follow this between the backs of houses, left, and a field on the right.

8 Cross a footbridge to the left and continue between gardens and a ditch on the right. Go through a gate, over another bridge to the right, over a stile ahead and diagonally left across a meadow behind the stone school and schoolhouse to a stile leading on to the road. Turn right to reach the church **A**.

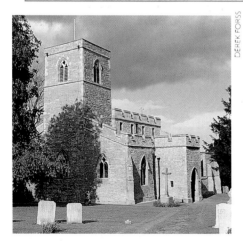

English preacher and writer.

THE RESTORED MILL

Stevington's 1770 postmill **D** revolved on a central pivot and was in full working order until about 1936. Then in 1951 the County Council carried out extensive restoration work to celebrate the Festival of Britain. The cloth-covered sails, which had to be controlled by hand in windy conditions, were replaced in 1957. It is thought that an earlier mill known as Miller's Piece stood nearer Turvey and the railway line, on higher ground.

▶ *Honey-coloured houses and cottages and the impressive church of St Mary (left) are attractive features in Stevington.*

BUTTERFLY GRASSLANDS

On an outcrop of the Chiltern Hills through downlands and valleys

Dunstable Downs **A** provides a spectacular starting point for this varied walk. Rising to nearly 800 feet (244 metres), the Downs are the highest point in Bedfordshire.

Near the car park the high mound of Five Knolls, a group of Neolithic or early Bronze Age burial mounds, can be seen to the right. Far over on the left is the outcrop of Ivinghoe Beacon, the site of an Iron Age settlement, and the ancient Icknield Way passes close by.

Whipsnade Zoo **B** can be visited at Stage 2 of the walk by crossing the car park to the entrance on the B4540, just past Whipsnade Green.

The walk passes a tree 'cathedral' **C**, a natural 'cathedral' planted with over 25 different varieties of trees.

FACT FILE

- ☀ Dunstable Downs on the B4541, 1 mile (1.6 km) south of Dunstable

- Pathfinder 1095 (TL 01/11) and 1094 (SP 81/91), grid reference TL 009197

miles 0 1 2 3 4 5 6 7 8 9 10 miles
kms 0 1 2 3 4 5 6 7 8 9 10 11 12 13 14 15 kms

- 🕐 2 hours

- Can become rutted and muddy on the bridleways; stout shoes are recommended

- **P** Information Centre

- **T** Bus service: contact Bedford (01234) 228337 for details

- The Chequers and the Old Hunter's Lodge at Whipsnade

- 🍴 Refreshment kiosk at the Information Centre

- **WC**

▶ *The interior of St Mary Magdalene's church in the village of Whipsnade. The simple but elegant nave is early 18th-century, built with local brick.*

▲*The chalk grasslands of Dunstable Downs are inhabited by plants which encourage a wide range of butterflies. There are at least 30 species in the area, including the red admiral (inset).*

This unusual feature was the brainchild of Mr E K Blyth, who decided to commemorate the deaths of three of his friends in World War I. Planting began in 1930 and it was given to the National Trust in 1969.

St Mary Magdalene church **D** in Whipsnade has a late 16th-century tower built in local brick, with fine bells which have fostered a tradition of bell ringing. The splendidly carved pulpit with its steps, door and tester is 17th-century.

Handwritten note:

Dear (Amphill all road)
The Whipsnade – D. Downs
walk looks OK
– or we could on past of
the ~~Ridgway~~ Ridgway where
I knew this little pub but we
would have to return the same way

WHIPSNADE DUNSTABLE DOWNS

The walk begins a park and Informa at Dunstable Dow the B4541.

1 From the car Information Centr Dunstable Downs down over the gra area of hawthorn s Turn left and walk the edge of the bus there is no clear pat marked, but keep along the side of the hill with the valley down on the right. The route then goes ahead into trees along a well-trodden path, which comes out at a gate into a meadow. Go through and keep walking ahead through the middle of this long narrow meadow. When the meadow meets woodland go through a gate in the middle of the fence here.

2 Walk ahead onto a wide track that leads from Bison Hill car park. Before reaching this, bear left up a track that leads along the edge of an open grassy triangle bearing slightly left into a tree-lined, old hollow way. Near a red-brick bungalow, a hole in the hedge on the right leads into Whipsnade Zoo **B** car park. For Zoo details, telephone Whipsnade (01582) 872171.

3 To continue the walk, turn left just past the bungalow along a signposted footpath and follow the track to the 'National Trust Whipsnade' sign. Cross the stile here and keep ahead along the edge of a field (the hollows in the field show signs of old chalk workings). Cross the stile at the end of the

... lane opposite, past houses, bearing right to The Chequers pub. Take a left turn immediately past the pub, down a small lane lined with hazelnut trees.

5 Just before the lane widens out, where a slip road comes in, turn left through the hedge (signposted). Carry on along the edge of a meadow with the unusual conifers of Heath Wood on the horizon to the right, passing a deep chalk pit on the left. Cross a stile, go on a short way to a footpath signpost and cross another stile to the left, walking along the edge of a meadow towards Whipsnade church **D**. Cross the stile into the churchyard and walk to the front and out onto another green.

6 Walk to the right down the road, past the 17th-century Old Rectory on the right and the Old Hunter's Lodge pub on the left, to the crossroads. Cross the Dunstable road onto Whipsnade Heath where there is a car park.

7 At the back of the car park go through wooden fencing and take a diagonal path slightly to the left through woodland, ignoring all side paths. The path leaves the wood through a

fence and continues along the edge of a field to a stile. Cross this and continue ahead through the middle of a field and across another stile to the road.

8 Turn left along the road past two bungalows, then take the next lane to the left (Land Park Lane).

9 At the main road, turn left for a short distance and look for a public bridleway sign on the right. Follow this bridleway right and when it comes out onto a crosstrack, bear left downhill to where the main track goes left.

10 Turn right here along another bridleway which skirts along the back of

mobile homes, then passes through meadows and woods. The track passes a radio mast on the left, then crosses a farm roadway and continues on along the edge of a wood on the left to a gate leading into a meadow by a National Trust sign.

11 This is the same meadow that you crossed on the outward journey, but instead of returning through the middle, turn right and go along the top edge to a gate at the far side. Go through the gate and turn left to another gate into the meadow. Turn right by this to retrace the route back to the car park.

◄ *This exotic building is in the Swiss Garden, which was created in the 19th century. The garden, run by Bedford council, includes ponds, arbours, a fernery and many other features. The shaggy parasol mushroom (above) is edible, but can smell offputting.*

cloaks to add to the picturesque nature of the scene. The estate was sold in 1871 to the Shuttleworth family, whose influence lasted until after World War II. They replaced the old house in 1872 with a mansion in the park designed by Clutton (now Shuttleworth Agricultural College **B**), which can be seen at various points of the walk.

ABBEY PEARS

The walk leaves the village street along a footpath that leads to St Leonard's Church **C**. Originally the church was attached to Warden Abbey, a Cistercian foundation on the outskirts of the village, famous for its Warden pears. This mainly 14th-century building has 12th-century work at the bottom of the tower. The interior is full of magnificent carved woodwork (including a gallery) brought back by the third

From a show village and an aircraft museum to a 19th-century garden

This walk explores the lovely village of Old Warden and its surrounding countryside of hills, fields and woods, formerly part of the Old Warden Park estate. The long-distance Greens and Ridge walk passes through here.

To begin with, the walk skirts Old Warden airfield, home of the Shuttleworth Collection **A**. This museum of early aircraft is a memorial to Richard Shuttleworth, of nearby Old Warden Park, who was killed in World War II. The public footpath leads through the middle of farmland, bordering a small stream. The stream runs from the fishing lake of the neighbouring estate of Southill Park, home of the Whitbread brewing family.

After passing through the woods of Warden Warren, you arrive in the village street. Here the influence of two families who owned the estates in Old Warden is visible in the decoration of the former estate houses — the cottages are stylized and ornate, built with a variety of ornamental touches such as decorative thatch or ridge tiles, bargeboarding and fancy porches. Most of the early cottages were built by the family who were in residence at Old Warden Park from the late 17th to the late 19th centuries. Lord Ongley required his tenants to wear tall hats and red

FACT FILE

* Old Warden, 4 miles (6 km) west of Biggleswade

* Pathfinder 1025 (TL 04/14), grid reference TL 150448

  miles 0 1 2 3 4 5 6 7 8 9 10 miles
  kms 0 1 2 3 4 5 6 7 8 9 10 11 12 13 14 15 kms

* 1½ hours

* Fairly flat; field paths can be somewhat overgrown

* **P** Swiss Garden car park almost opposite the entrance to the Shuttleworth Collection

* Hare and Hounds in Old Warden

* **I** The Swiss Garden is open from January to the end of October, Tel. (01582) 471012 for times. The Shuttleworth Collection of historic aircraft and vintage cars is open daily: April to October 10.00am–4.00pm, November to March 10.00am–3.00pm. Flying display first Monday of every month. Tel: (01767) 627288. Admission charge

THE WALK

OLD WARDEN

The walk begins at the Swiss Garden car park, almost opposite the Shuttleworth Collection Ⓐ.

1 Leave the car park via the main entrance and turn left along the road, taking care as the road can become quite busy at weekends.

2 After some distance, where the road bears left over a stream, turn right along a signposted public bridleway along the edge of a field with the stream on the right. Old Warden airfield stretches away beyond the stream, with a view of Shuttleworth House Ⓑ beyond. The path follows the curves of the field, then crosses a green-painted bridge to the right through a gate. Turn left again on the other bank to continue following the stream, which is now on the left. Go through another gate and turn left over a wooden bridge, turning right on the other side to continue following the stream, which is now on the right. Pass a small lake and go through a gate to walk ahead through a field to another gate on the far side.

3 Go through the gate and turn right along an estate road for a short distance, turn left into a field (signposted) and follow it to the right, along the edge of the stream on the right. At the end of the field turn left to the exit just a few paces along. Continue ahead along a wide grassy track beside the edge of a field with new woods on the right. At the end of the woods the track continues through the middle of the field to exit onto a small road through a metal farm gate.

4 Turn right along the road past the beautiful woods of the Southill estate on the left, which in summer almost hide the wide expanse of a fishing lake.

5 Turn right off the road through a white gate, just past a pretty, thatched lodge cottage, along a broad track leading through mixed conifers. When the hard track bears off to the right, carry on ahead along a grassy track (arrow on post) that leads down through woods and bracken onto the main street of Old Warden, opposite a pump building.

6 Turn left along the road past the Hare and Hounds pub on the left of the Post Office. Opposite this is a thatched cottage, which has on its side gable a mailed hand clutching a shuttle (the Shuttleworth insignia).

7 Just past the cottage turn right up a signposted track, with a wall on the right and a field on the left. This leads up steps and ahead through a field to an iron kissing gate. Go through this and ahead through another field, through a second kissing gate to the church Ⓒ. From this elevated position there are good views of Shuttleworth House and its lake.

8 Leave the church by the main gate and turn left down a lane to the main road.

9 Turn left along the road past a thatched pump building to the Old Carpenter's workshop on the right.

10 Opposite this turn left up a farm road. When the road swings left, turn right into a field through a gate (signposted) and walk along the edge of the field beside a barbed wire fence on the left, finally bearing right towards a small white gate.

11 Go through this and turn left along the road past the turning to Ickwell and Northill. The entrance to the Swiss Garden Ⓓ comes up shortly on the right. Opposite is a path that will lead you back to the car park and the starting point of the walk.

Lord Ongley from his travels in Europe. Some of the woodwork, marked with the initials AC under a crown, is said to have come from Anne of Cleves' chapel in Bruges. The first Baron Ongley of Old Warden, ennobled because of his political career, left money for a substantial family mausoleum to be built in the churchyard. Nearby is the Shuttleworth family vault.

A fitting ending to this walk is a visit to the Swiss Garden Ⓓ, now in the care of Bedfordshire County Council. It was created in the early 19th century around a Swiss chalet rumoured to have housed a Swiss mistress. The 8 acres (3 hectares) of the garden are designed in the Romantic style with shrubberies, aerial trellises for climbing plants, ponds, arbours, glades and winding paths leading to various Victorian features, including a grotto and fernery, a 'chapel' or garden house, a summerhouse and a well. The Shuttleworth family further developed the garden and now the interesting trees and shrubs play host to a large variety of wildlife.

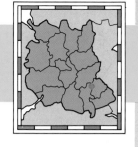

A walk from a lovely stone-built village set in a verdant valley

The village of Turvey plays host to some attractive features. Its houses and cottages are built from a mellow limestone and there is a mill complete with millpond, as well as a Saxon church. At the western edge of the village is the oldest stone bridge in Bedfordshire, spanning the lazy River Great Ouse.

This walk explores the village, once famous for its lace-making, and takes a detour into the surrounding countryside, from which its favoured position, surrounded by parkland in the lush valley of the Ouse, can best be appreciated.

SPLENDID IRONWORK

You start in a square by the War Memorial, the Three Cranes pub and All Saints Church Ⓐ. You enter the churchyard and pass through a lychgate set in billowing yew hedges. Huge black oak doors embellished with some splendid 13th-century ironwork — probably by John of Leighton, who also worked on Westminster Abbey — lead into the interior that was

restored by Sir Gilbert Scott in 1852. Saxon work can still be seen in the rounded arches high on the south wall of the nave and in the tower, and there is a 13th-century wall painting of the Crucifixion in the lady chapel. There are also four interesting 16th-century monuments to members of the Mordaunt family, the lords of the manor from the 13th to the 18th century.

FINE VIEWS

Leaving town, you pass Chantry Farm, with its ecclesiastical buildings and thick yew hedges, then follow the boundary of the late Georgian Turvey House Ⓑ, which is set in lovely parkland dotted with mature trees. The climb gives good views back into the town as you head east along a bridleway. Across fields to the north is St Mary's Ⓒ, the parish church of Carlton, though it stands outside the village.

You descend along a bridleway through fields to a main road, then cross into woods and meadowland. As you return to Turvey, you pass a Jacobean manor house known as Turvey Abbey Ⓓ. The house took its

▲ *Turvey's impressive, 13th-century stone bridge has eleven arches spanning the River Great Ouse. The common hawker dragonfly (inset) restlessly hovers over reedy stretches of river.*

name from the Benedictine abbey of Bec, in Normandy, which once owned the land, but it was not used by a religious order until recently — it now houses Benedictine nuns.

Beyond the Abbey, down the main road, is a lovely square of 17th-century workers' houses, but our route goes through meadows and woodland to the Great Ouse, where two statues, known locally as Jonah and his wife, stand in the millpond in front of the massive bulk of the renovated mill. 'Jonah' once stood outside Ashridge House and was brought here in 1844. The head and body of his wife were found at the mill and assembled to join Jonah in the pond in 1953.

Nearby are Turvey's 11-arched, 13th-century bridge Ⓔ and the 17th-century Ye Three Fyshes Inn. One of Guy Fawkes' co-conspirators in the Gunpowder Plot (1605) was arrested here. The pub has paid a price for its

---

FACT FILE

☀ Turvey, 7½ miles (12km) west of Bedford

▱ Pathfinder 1001 (SP 85/95), grid reference SP 941524

miles 0 1 2 3 4 5 6 7 8 9 10 miles
kms 0 1 2 3 4 5 6 7 8 9 10 11 12 13 14 15 kms

◐ 2¼ hours

▬ Some gentle slopes; roads and paths may be muddy in wet weather

Ⓟ In small square by Turvey's church

▦ The Three Cranes pub, Three Fyshes Inn, King's Arms pub and Laws Hotel, all located in Turvey

---

DEREK FORSS. INSET: E.T.HOMPSON/AQUILA

THE WALK

TURVEY – CARLTON SCHOOL

The walk starts in Turvey by All Saints Church Ⓐ, just off the A428 on a byroad signposted to Carlton.

1 Turn left up Carlton Road, passing the post office on your left and the Old Rectory on your right. Turvey House Ⓑ lies beyond the stone wall on your left. Continue along the wide verge on the left-hand side of this long, straight road.

2 Just before a point where the road bends to the left, turn to the right along a signposted bridleway with a hedge on your left. After nearly ½ mile (800m), go through a gateway and bear half-left towards Northey Farm.

3 Cross a stile and turn right to go through the farmyard along a small roadway. The Church of St Mary Ⓒ lies away to your left. Continue past houses belonging to Carlton School.

4 At a bridleway sign, turn right down a wide country track. Follow it past stabling, then downhill across fields until you reach a farm track leading back to Great Oaks Farm.

5 Turn right through the gate by the cattle grid and continue down the track to a main road.

6 Cross and continue down a bridleway signposted to Astwood. Just before a wooden gateway, turn right to walk along a narrow leafy path, going alongside a stream on the right.

7 Cross a small wooden footbridge and turn immediately right along a small, unmarked track through a strip of scrub. Cross a fence to enter parkland. Walk ahead roughly parallel to the main road (there is no clear path here) to reach a section of wooden fencing and a stile crossing a wire fence. Continue walking straight on towards a concrete bridge over a stream, where a signpost points across the next stretch of meadow. Make for the road near a new wooden building and conifers.

8 Go through a wooden kissing-gate and turn left to go along the road past Turvey Abbey Ⓓ.

9 Turn left down Jacks Lane, past the Kings Arms pub, along a cinder track. Go through a gate to come to a three-pronged, public footpath signpost in parkland.

10 Turn right and cross a stile into woodland. Continue, across stiles and meadows, to a wide green lane with a stream on the right. Go through a gateway onto Newton's Lane, with a cottage called The Old Lace School on the left and Nell's Well just to the right.

11 Cross the lane, going a little to the left, then ahead into a housing estate. Bear right and carry on down the tarmac footpath to some old cottages. Bear right past the renovated mill to the Three Fyshes pub on the left. Turn left to the bridge Ⓔ.

12 Return up the main road to the Central Stores Ⓕ, and return to the start.

picturesque setting; several flood gauges set into the wall testify to periodic inundations.

Walking back along the main road, you reach the Central Stores. The building, whose structure was altered in 1840, was once a coaching inn called The Tinker of Turvey Ⓕ, which dated back to 1150. The inn sign, featuring the tinker, Old Nell, his wife, and their dog, is now in Luton Museum. Inside the Stores, there are iron rings in the walls, where prisoners destined for Bedford Gaol were shackled while waiting to change coaches.

▶ *The Great Ouse meanders lazily through the parkland of Turvey House, an elegant late Georgian manor house.*

ANIMAL FARM

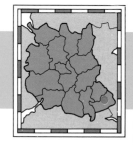

PAUL FELIX. INSET: A. BARNES/NHPA

A walk around the setting of George Orwell's satirical novel

Wallington is a small village, tucked away in the folds of Hertfordshire. Its chief claim to fame is its connection with the writer George Orwell, though it is known locally for its duck ponds.

Its church, the 500-year-old St Mary's **Ⓐ**, has retained much of its original 15th-century structure, including a north aisle roof which is held up by carved angels, a wooden screen and stained glass showing the arms of the Priscot family in the north chapel above a table tomb. Sir John Priscot, who died in 1460, was Judge of Common Pleas and Lord of the Manor of Wallington.

The walk leaves the church and goes along a wooded green lane to reach Wallington Common Nature Reserve **Ⓑ**, an ancient wood where roe deer can often be seen. It is a fascinating area of ancient trees,

FACT FILE

☀ St Mary's church, Wallington, 5 miles (8 km) east of Baldock. Turn left off A507 to Buntingford at a roundabout on the outskirts of Baldock

🗺 Pathfinder 1049 (TL 23/33), grid reference TL 292335

```
miles 0   1   2   3   4   5   6   7   8   9   10 miles
kms   0 1 2 3 4 5 6 7 8 9 10 11 12 13 14 15 kms
```

◔ 2½ hours

▬ Reasonable, but some tracks can be rutted and muddy at times

🅿 Limited parking by St Mary's church, reached by turning right up a lane off the main street at a bend by a pond

🍺 The Moon and Stars at Rushden

▶ *Manor Farm in Wallington is said to have been the inspiration for Orwell's satirical novel* Animal Farm.

▲ *Despite the fact that world-renowned author George Orwell lived there, Wallington is more famous locally for its duck ponds. The wren (inset) is happy to nest in nearby hedges.*

adorned with violets, primroses and bluebells in spring. Dog's mercury grows in abundance.

On the wall of the Old Forge in Redhill, there is a plaque commemorating the 19th-century sickle manufacturer James Field. The

PAUL FELIX

THE WALK

WALLINGTON – SHAW GREEN

The walk starts at St Mary's church Ⓐ, Wallington.

1 Turn right out of the churchyard and walk down the wide track away from Wallington Bury Farm buildings, past an ivy-covered wall and the fence of the imposing red-brick rectory on the right.

2 At a junction of tracks bear left on a public bridleway signposted to Wallington Common, a wide tree-lined green lane. The buildings of Bury Farm are over the field on the left. Follow along the tree-lined track which bends first to the left, then to the right until it opens up into Wallington Common Ⓑ.

3 Pass a pond on the left and at a Nature Reserve board bear left and follow the rutted track along by a small ditch and raised bank on the left. Keep following the gently twisting track as it leaves Wallington Common and carry on to a crosstrack.

4 Turn left along this towards a farm house. Keep going straight ahead between farm buildings and Shaw Green Farmhouse on the right, and turn slightly through more farm buildings to a yard littered with farm implements.

5 Turn left at the edge of

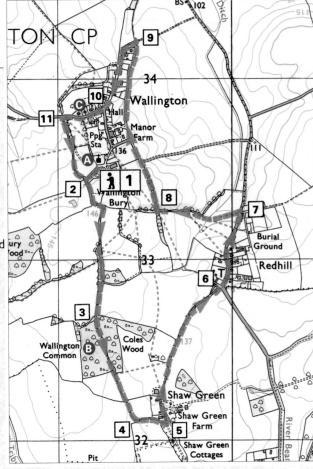

the yard, almost doubling back in the direction of the Common and Coles Wood, and walking ahead along a broad green track towards a copse. Pass this copse and then a pond on the left. Keep straight on ahead between hedges towards the houses of Redhill. Walk between houses onto the main road.

6 At the main road, turn left. (For refreshment turn right at the main road. Carry on up the road for ½ mile (800 metres) to the Moon and Stars pub in Rushden, then return to junction.) Walk through the village past houses and

cottages old and new, ignoring various footpath signs to the left. Continue to the end of the village.

7 Near the end of the village turn left along a signposted footpath opposite a thatched cottage. This footpath takes you across the middle of a field. Walk ahead towards two trees which mark the line of a ditch. Cross a wooden footbridge. Continue on across an open section of field, then go straight on along the edge of the field with trees and scrub on your right-hand side.

8 The path arrives at the

meeting place of farm tracks, hedges and knots of trees. Turn right along the edge of a field here with a hedgerow on the left and a good view over a sweep of open countryside on the right. The track comes out onto a road at a bend. Continue ahead up the road a short way to another bend. Go straight on along a signposted bridleway. The rutted track to Manor Farm swings left but the walk continues along a wide green track ahead. On the right is a field and on the left you will find the gardens of Wallington.

9 At a crosstrack, turn sharp left back towards the village, bear left and continue up the street.

10 At the road junction by the former Plough pub, opposite the village hall with its splendid clock, turn right to Kits Lane where the first cottage Ⓒ on the right bears a plaque commemorating Orwell. Continue on up Kits Lane to the brow of the hill crowned with lovely stands of beech trees.

11 Turn left along a signposted bridleway past a pretty brick cottage on the left. Continue on by the grounds of the rectory to a junction of tracks. Turn left back towards the church and parking place.

PAUL FELIX

almost hidden burial ground on the right is the site of the earliest non-conformist chapel in Hertfordshire, dating from 1720.

The writer George Orwell moved to a 300-year-old cottage Ⓒ in Kits Lane from lodgings in Wigan in April 1936. It had formerly been the

◄The path from Shaw Green Farm can be a little overgrown in early summer, especially after a damp spring.

village shop and he reopened the shop in the afternoons to help pay the rent. The mornings were reserved for writing. He lived here on and off for four years. *The Road to Wigan Pier*, Orwell's study of northern working-class life, and *Homage to Catalonia*, describing his few months fighting in the Spanish Civil War, were written during this time. In June 1936 he married Eileen O'Shaunessy in the local church.

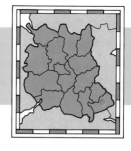
HERTFORDSHIRE

Along a disused railway through a rural area with unspoilt villages

Although this west corner of Hertfordshire is not far from the busy A1, the parkland of Brocket Hall and the surrounding countryside of rolling fields and woods with small, scattered settlements of old houses give the impression that not much has changed in several hundred years. The walk starts at the hamlet of Waterend on the River Lea. Here the Jacobean Waterend House **Ⓐ** (dated 1610) with its splendid ornamental brick chimneys is said to be the birthplace of Sarah Jennings (1660-1744), later Duchess of Marlborough and confidante

FACT FILE

- ☀ Waterend, 3 miles (4.8 km) south of Hatfield

- ⌖ Pathfinders 1095 (TL 01/11) and 1096 (TL 21/31), grid reference TL 203138

miles 0 1 2 3 4 5 6 7 8 9 10 miles
kms 0 1 2 3 4 5 6 7 8 9 10 11 12 13 14 15 kms

- ◔ 2½ hours

- ▭ Reasonably flat; muddy in places in wet weather

- P Near the ford at Waterend

- T Bus from Wheathampstead or Welwyn

- ▥ The Waggoner's at Ayot Green. Pubs at Lemsford

of Queen Anne. One of its lovely old barns has been taken down and reconstructed as a restaurant in the centre of St Albans.

RAILWAY TRACK

The path leaves the river, turning through fields to join the track of a former railway, now a pleasant recreational path called the Ayot Greenway **Ⓑ**, administered by Hertfordshire County Council. The cuttings and embankments of this

▲*The village green at Ayot Green. The vivid red and black colours of the cinnabar moth (inset) give a warning to predators — birds, lizards and mammals — that they are poisonous.*

2½ mile (4 km) path provide a variety of excellent habitats for flowers, birds and butterflies and offer lovely views over the surrounding countryside. Much of the line is wooded with a pleasant mixture of hardwood trees. Clearings and coppiced

DAVID HUGHES. INSET: M.I. GARWOOD/NHPA

THE WALK

WATEREND – AYOT GREEN – LEMSFORD

The walk begins by the ford at Waterend. Leave the A1 at Junction 4 signposted to Hertford, Hatfield and Welwyn Garden City. Follow the signs to Welwyn Garden City (A6129) then take the Wheathampstead road (B653). After about 2 miles (3.2 km) take a tiny right-hand turn to Waterend and Ayot Green just after a picnic place marked by a 'P' sign on the right-hand side of the road.

▶ Cross over the ford via the footbridge and turn left down the bridleway opposite Waterend House Ⓐ signposted to Wheathampstead (Lea Valley Walk).

▶ When this broad track divides, turn up the right fork which shortly reaches the old railway (now the Ayot Greenway Ⓑ) just by Robinson's Wood.

▶ Turn right along the old railway track which is broad and firm underfoot; it runs through pastoral scenery with some pleasant views from flower-strewn embankments and is lined with trees that create a dappled tunnel effect when the track goes through a cutting. There are useful benches at intervals and cross paths are marked with wooden marker posts.

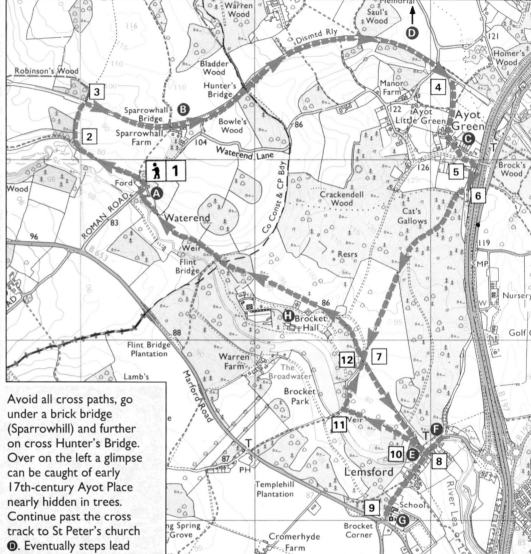

Avoid all cross paths, go under a brick bridge (Sparrowhill) and further on cross Hunter's Bridge. Over on the left a glimpse can be caught of early 17th-century Ayot Place nearly hidden in trees. Continue past the cross track to St Peter's church Ⓓ. Eventually steps lead down to a road near a road junction.

▶ Go ahead down the road signposted to Ayot Green Ⓒ and walk past pleasant houses onto the green itself, shaded by huge old trees. A glimpse of St Peter's church can be seen from here. Keep on bearing slightly to the left to the road bridge over the A1.

▶ Just before the bridge, turn right down Brickwall Close to the Waggoner's pub in Ayot Green.

▶ Opposite the pub turn right over a stile in a fence into Brocket Park by a

◀ *The imposing Waterend House, encountered at the beginning of the walk in the hamlet of Waterend, was built in 1610 in the architectural style of the Jacobean period.*

areas provide different conditions for the wildlife. This railway, once used by George Bernard Shaw (who lived at nearby Ayot St Lawrence) to journey to London, was axed by Dr Beeching in 1965.

SHADY OAKS

From the railway track it is just a short stroll down a lane to the pretty village of Ayot Green Ⓒ. The attractive cottages that surround the notice board. The path bears round to the left skirting a pond to another stile. Cross this, passing a small brick cottage on the left, and follow the broad path through the mainly conifer woods going sharply downhill at one stage. The track diverges; keep to the left-hand branch marked with a yellow arrow on a wooden post (all the footpaths on the Brocket estate are well marked in a similar manner). The track crosses another path and then goes over a stile onto a new golf course. Continue straight across the golf course (watching out for stray golf balls) in the general direction of a tall spindly pine rising from woodland ahead.

7 At the estate road near

a white-striped sleeping policeman turn sharp left to follow the waymarks across the golf course to a stile in a fence. Cross this and continue across some grass onto a small roadway. Cross the River Lea on a metal footbridge with the imposing bulk of Lemsford Mill **E** over on the right.

8 Turn left for a short detour to see old Bridge House next to the Sun pub, old cottages, the Long and Short Arm pub and Lemsford Springs nature reserve **F** close by.

9 Retrace your steps and walk up the road for some way on another detour past beautiful Mill House to visit the church of St John the Evangelist **G**. Retrace your steps.

10 Go back down the

road to Lemsford and turn left back over the bridge near the mill and this time walk to the left along a wire mesh fence (signposted). Cross a stile onto Brocket Hall golf course again and continue straight ahead following the waymarks until the bridge comes into sight. From the bridge there is a lovely view of Brocket Hall **H** overlooking the lake.

11 Do not cross over the bridge, but to continue the walk turn back along the driveway towards Brocket Hall. Follow the waymarks along the edge of the golf course to reach the point near the sleeping policeman where earlier the walk branched off to Lemsford.

12 Turn left over the

roadway here, over a fence and along a good fenced track, with a hedge on the left partially screening the back of Brocket Hall. Cross a stile, go over a small road, cross another stile to the left and walk through the middle of a field studded with magnificent parkland trees following the arrowed posts. The stable block with its cupola is on the left. Follow the marker posts towards a wood. Cross a stile into the wood continuing on along the clear track through it. Carry straight on along the track, which leads back to Waterend passing alongside the garden of Waterend House on the right and the river on the left until you arrive back at the ford.

ALL PHOTOS DAVID HUGHES

◀*Sparrow Hill bridge crosses the Ayot Greenway path that runs along the track of a disused railway.*

▶*The listed brick and weather-boarded mill at Lemsford has been restored and converted into offices.*

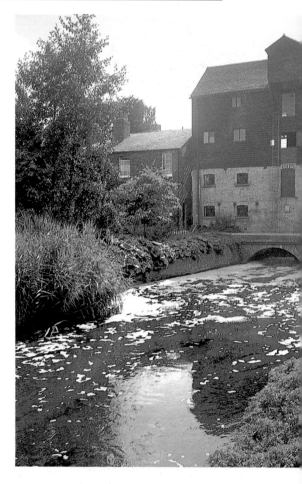

large green, shaded by huge oak and chestnut trees, were once homes for the workers on the nearby Brocket estate. One cottage was converted from an old, timber-framed toll-house built in 1728 to service the original route of the Great North Road. From the green you can see the red-brick broach spire of Ayot St Peter church **D**. It was built in 1874, the third church to serve the village, and is famous for its decoration of the Arts and Crafts movement.

From Ayot Green it is just a step into the grounds of Brocket Hall. The

path begins in mainly coniferous woodland which then opens out into grassy parkland dotted with fine mature trees, including several imposing cedars. A public right of way leads to Lemsford, emerging onto the village street near the brick and weather-boarded mill **E**. This listed building inspired the Victorian composer J P Skelly who was staying at Brocket Hall nearby when he wrote the song 'Nellie Dean'. It is said it was sung by soldiers destined for the Boer War who were billeted in the village.

▲*Rosebay willowherb grows in profusion in Brocket Park, the former estate of Brocket Hall, near Lemsford.*

Lemsford was originally on the direct route of the Great North Road and two former coaching inns still exist as pubs today: the old Sun Inn and the rebuilt Long and Short Arm. Lemsford Springs nature reserve ⑤

Illustrious Inhabitants of Brocket Hall

Peniston Lamb MP, First Viscount Melbourne, was a great society man who used Brocket Hall to throw magnificent parties. These included one in which he entertained the Prince Regent and had a race course created specially for the occasion.

The Second Viscount married Lady Caroline Ponsonby, daughter of Lord Bessborough. Beautiful, entertaining and a gifted author, she was also wild and unpredictable.

Her affairs scandalized society, especially her infatuation with the poet Lord Byron. The poet eventually rejected her in 1813, driving her to near despair.

Six years after her death Lord Melbourne became Queen Victoria's first Prime Minister. He died at Brocket Hall in 1848 and his tomb is in St Etheldreda's church at Hatfield. (The interesting Brocket chapel there contains tombs of earlier owners of Brocket Hall.)

A later inhabitant of more humble origins died at Brocket Hall in 1921. He was George Stephen, born in 1829 to a Scottish carpenter, who emigrated to Canada and made a vast fortune building the Canadian Pacific Railway. He became a peer — Lord Mount Stephen.

Brocket Hall, overlooking the bridge, was built in 1755. It is now a conference centre and is not generally open to the public.

COURTESY OF BROCKET HALL

is further on, past the pub. Here old watercress beds, willows and reeds offer an excellent habitat for birds. The wisteria-hung Mill House, 18th-century Bridge House and ancient cottages near the river as well as the two pubs all contribute to Lemsford's old-world charm.

CRAWLING GARGOYLES

A fairly short detour can be made to the main road to see the church of St John the Evangelist ⑥, which was built in 1859 by Earl Cowper close to the entrance gates to Brocket Hall. The Earl owned the nearby Panshanger estate and inherited the Brocket estate from his stepfather, Lord Palmerston. The stone church is in Early English style with a squat tower decorated with dragon gargoyles crawling down two corners.

The walk now re-enters the grounds of Brocket Hall ⑦ at the same point by the mill, but this time the footpath leads towards the

◀*This elegant bridge dating from 1772 was built to cross the River Lea in the grounds of the Brocket Hall estate.*

lovely waterfall and old bridge of 1772 over the River Lea and the nearby square red-brick mansion standing by the lake. The old Tudor house was demolished in 1746 when the estate was bought by Sir Matthew Lamb. In 1755 he commissioned James Paine to build his new mansion with magnificent interiors that provided a contrast with its plain exterior; Paine also designed the elegant old bridge.

LANDSCAPED GARDEN

Brocket Hall was home to two Prime Ministers: Lord Palmerston and his brother-in-law Lord Melbourne (whose wife was the beautiful and highly strung Lady Caroline Lamb). The grounds, after their initial layout, were later landscaped by Capability Brown with his inimitable clumps of trees and pastoral vistas. He created the lake by widening the River Lea. The Hall is now a conference centre and not generally open to the public; part of the park is now a golf course but the existing magnificent parkland trees have been retained.

PHOTOS GREAT BRITAIN.

tower, the church stands in a lonely position on the edge of the village. Nearby is Reed Hall, with its Tudor chimney and old moat.

EARLY SETTLERS

There are five other moats in the vicinity of the village, relics of ancient fortified houses. These bear mute witness to the former strategic importance of the village on the London to Cambridge road. Reed is one of the highest points in Hertfordshire and there were early settlements here, including a Roman camp, of which some physical evidence can still be seen.

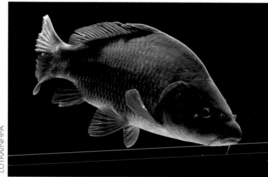

LUTRA/NHPA

◀ *Reed's church, in typical Hertfordshire style, has a flint and stone tower with brick window surrounds and parapets. The carp (above) has been farmed in fish-ponds since Roman times.*

A fortified village and a staging post in rural Hertfordshire

This walk through cultivated fields and woodland explores two villages. Reed is a hamlet of scattered houses built around three greens, and Barkway is a former market town full of interesting old buildings. They lie on an outcrop of the Chiltern Hills and are close to Ermine Street, a Roman road. Its route forms part of today's A10.

NORMAN DOORWAY

The walk starts at Reed's church **Ⓐ**, which has a blocked up Norman doorway. Built in flint, with a squat

FACT FILE

- ✳ Reed, 3 miles (4.8km) south of Royston

- 🗺 Pathfinder 1049 (TL 23/33), grid reference TL 361357

  miles 0 1 2 3 4 5 6 7 8 9 10 miles
  kms 0 1 2 3 4 5 6 7 8 9 10 11 12 13 14 15 kms

- ◕ Allow 2½ hours

- ▬ Can be overgrown in summer, when trousers and long sleeves are recommended. One section may be boggy after rain

- 🅿 On the wide verge outside Reed's church

- 🍴 The Chaise and Pair in Barkway and the Cabinet in Reed

Further on, Barkway's handsome High Street is a marvellous jumble of houses and cottages of every age, style and material. There are thatched roofs and tiled roofs; yellow brick, red brick, painted brick and plaster of every hue; jettied overhangs, exposed timbering, pargetting and flint walling.

One of the finest buildings is the thatched Berg Cottage **Ⓑ**, dated 1687. Opposite the red-brick Stallibrass Almshouses is a small yellow-brick building that in 1867 housed the slipper baths.

HIGHWAYMAN

Barkway stands on a former turnpike road from London to King's Lynn. Near a reed-fringed pond, the High Street widens where a market

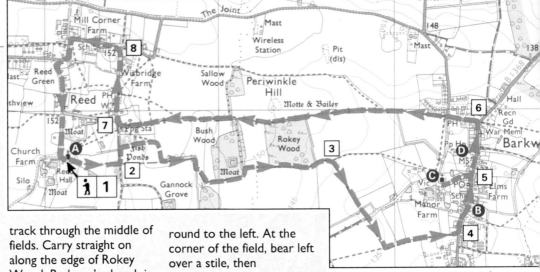

THE WALK

REED — BARKWAY

*The walk begins outside Reed's church **A**. Turn off the A10 about 2 miles (3.2km) to the south of Royston, then right by the recreation ground and straight on to the church.*

1 Leave the churchyard through a gap in the hedge to head east. Cross a plank footbridge and continue across the middle of a field towards a hedge.

2 Turn left along a crossing track, then right along a broad track, with a hedge containing mature trees on your left. At the end of the hedge, turn right along a wide farm track, bearing left at another hedge and trees, then right again. Follow the broad track to the left at a wood. Follow the edge of a large wood on your left (Bush Wood). Bear left round the end of the wood, then right again to leave the wood, still following this wide track through the middle of fields. Carry straight on along the edge of Rokey Wood. Barkway's church is visible in the trees ahead. The track passes between a hedge at the end of the wood and a row of young ash trees.

3 Continue on the track, which bears to the right, with a hedge on the left and a fence on the right. At a T-junction of paths, turn left for a short distance, looking out for a small, unsigned path at the corner of two hedges. This goes right, up a bank and into a field. Carry on along quite a wide track by a gappy hedge at the edge of the field. Follow the hedge round to the left. At the corner of the field, bear left over a stile, then immediately sharp right along a fenced path and over another stile.

4 When you reach Barkway High Street, turn left to pass Berg Cottage **B** on your right.

5 Take a small detour to the left to visit the church **C**. Return and continue along the High Street passing the milestone **D**.

6 Turn left down the road to Reed and Royston. Where the road bends to the right, continue straight ahead along a signposted byway. Continue on the wide, grassy track through fields, passing Rokey Wood on your left. Cross a broad farm track and continue along an overgrown green lane to a cross track.

7 Turn right to the road and cross it to pass the Cabinet pub, continuing to the next road junction.

8 Turn left down Jackson's Lane and left at the next junction down Blacksmith's Lane. Follow the road round then turn left by the recreation ground into Church Lane, which leads back to the starting point.

---

used to be held. Opposite Church Lane are two three-storey coaching inns. The village even had its own highwayman, Thomas Flack, who was hanged in 1747.

Down the side lane opposite the old forge, past the horsepond, lies the Church of St Mary Magdalene **C**, which contains some interesting memorials to various local people. In the main, these are dedicated to the inhabitants of two big houses in the area, Newsells and Cokenach.

Under the tower is a memorial to Admiral Sir John Jennings (who died in 1743) by the famous sculptor, Rysbrack. It was originally intended for Westminster Abbey but was too big for its allotted space.

LORD OF THE MANOR

There is also a brass of 1561 to Robert Poynard and family, and a floor slab in memory of Henry Prannell, lord of the manor in 1599, who married Frances Howard, granddaughter of the Dukes of Norfolk and Buckingham and later the Countess of Hertford.

◄ *Hedgerows with mature trees, as here near Bush Wood, are a feature of the farmland stretches on this walk.*

PHOTOS GREAT BRITAIN

Further up the High Street is the last and most decorative milestone **D** of a number set up going out of Cambridge by Dr William Warren, Master of Trinity Hall, in about 1725. The money came from a bequest to the college from two Elizabethan Fellows, whose coats of arms, together with those of Trinity Hall, decorate the milestones. Those on the first milestone out of Cambridge (at Trumpington) are of Dr Mouse, a former Master, while those on Barkway's 5-foot (1.5-m) milestone are of the second benefactor, Mr Hare, a friend and executor of Dr Mouse.

MOTTE AND BAILEY

The walk returns through woods and farmland, passing the almost indistinguishable remains of a motte and bailey. Finally, the route leads around the village of Reed, whose houses are separated by several pretty greens, to return to the start.

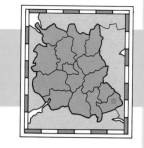

DEREK PRATT. INSET: J & M BAIN/NHPA

▲*A view through fields of yellow rape across the valley of the River Beane. Cuckoo pint (left), also known as lords and ladies or wild arum, flourishes in damp, shady hedgerow bottoms.*

FACT FILE

* Walkern, 4 miles (6.4km) east of Stevenage

* Pathfinder 1073 (TL 22/32), grid reference TL 290266

miles 0 1 2 3 4 5 6 7 8 9 10 miles
kms 0 1 2 3 4 5 6 7 8 9 10 11 12 13 14 15 kms

* Allow 3 hours

* Gentle slopes; field paths and woodland. Muddy in winter or after rain

* P In the village street near Church Lane, or outside the church (park carefully as the lane is narrow)

* The Robin Hood, Yew Tree and White Lion pubs in Walkern, and the Bell pub in Benington

* Benington Lordship is open at limited times between April and September, Tel. (01438) 869668 for details

Through the fields and woods connecting two charming villages

The gently rolling, wooded countryside of the Beane Valley provides a beautiful setting for this walk. The route follows old green ways and footpaths linking the exceptionally pretty village of Benington with its larger, but equally interesting neighbour, Walkern.

Normally, the water meadows at the bottom of the valley frame the clear waters of the River Beane, but due to a lowering of the water table after several dry years in this area,

springs have dried up and the Beane is a mere shadow of its former self. Some of the many ponds passed on the walk are also at worryingly low levels.

The walk begins near Hertfordshire's oldest church, St Mary the Virgin Ⓐ in Walkern. Founded at the beginning of the 11th century, it has a Saxon nave and doorway, and a stone rood figure in an early Norman aisle. There are some interesting brasses and monuments — that of a 13th-century knight with

▼*It is well worth making a short detour to the village of Ardeley, which has some very attractive buildings.*

DEREK PRATT

THE WALK

WALKERN – BENINGTON

The walk begins at the junction of Church End and the main street in Walkern (the B1037).

1 Go down Church End, over the ford, and past the church **A** on your left.

2 A little beyond a lane on your right signposted to Bassus Green, turn left on a signposted footpath by a house. Cross a stile and bear diagonally right over a bumpy meadow, ignoring the path straight ahead. Pass to the left of a pond.

3 At a stile, cross and bear left along the field edge, with a hedgerow and trees on your left. The track bears slightly right, then left round the end of a ditch. Continue on ahead through a strip of woodland where a hedge and ditch come in from your right.

4 Bear slightly right down the edge of the next field, with an old metal fence and hedge on your right. Go over a barred stile to the right of a metal gate ahead and continue alongside the metal fence. Go through a metal gate and continue following the fence, beyond which is Ardeley Bury **B**. Walk through two wooden gates, taking the path over a stream, then leave the metal fence and go across the field to the far right-hand corner. Go over a stile and through bushes to the road.

5 To make a detour into Ardeley village, go down the lane ahead. Otherwise, turn right along a concrete track signposted to Wood End. This becomes a deeply rutted, muddy green lane, and comes out into a

field. Continue ahead, gently uphill, along the hedge on your right. Go through a belt of trees to a cross track at the corner of the field. The left turn leads to Wood End, but you bear right along a farm track to a metal signpost near another cross track. Bear left downhill. Walkern Bury Farm is on the slope ahead; trees mask the site of an ancient ring and bailey **C** behind it. Walk uphill, turn right at a driveway and continue until you come to a road.

6 Turn left to Bassus Green. Turn right at the crossroads. Where the lane bends left by woods, turn right on a signposted bridleway. Continue down and then up this broad muddy track, with woods on your left and open fields on your right, towards the buildings of Walkern Hall Farm. The track meets a road opposite Walkern Hall **D**.

7 Turn right past a duck pond, then left down the bridleway to Benington

(signposted 'Circular Walk'). Go through metal gates to pass Walkern Hall on your left. Go through more metal gates onto a tree-lined, concrete driveway. Walk down to a gatehouse on your left and Box Hall on your right.

8 Turn left down Walkern Road to Benington village green. Bear right to the church **E** and the entrance to Benington Lordship **F**.

9 Return past the green to the village hall, then turn left through a waymarked metal kissing-gate

signposted to Aston End. Leave a fence on your left, and bear slightly to the left across a meadow. Benington Bury can be seen through trees on your right and the gardens and house of the Lordship on your left. Cross a barred stile and carry on through the next meadow to a metal gate, a bridge over a stream and then a stile into the next field. Keep ahead

ALL PHOTOS: DEREK PRATT

◄Between Ardeley and Benington the route passes close to Walkern Hall, an interesting Regency mansion.

a traditional English village. The old Bell pub, built in similar style, boasts an early 18th-century wall painting in its bar.

Nearby, St Peter's Church **E** is set in a lovely, flowery churchyard. The huge contorted yew near the church door is said to be 1,000 years old. The present church was built by John de Benstede, Keeper of the Great Seal and of the Wardrobe to Edward I, who owned the manor in 1285. Later additions and embellishments were carried out by his descendants. The Benstede coat of arms can be seen on the tower, in some windows and also in the

his face hidden by a visor is one of only three similar in the whole of England — and a late 14th-century font. In the churchyard, there is a fine memorial, dating from around 1765, to a Susannah Lewis.

The route leaves the village to circle towards Benington by way of Ardeley Bury **B**, an Elizabethan house restored in the Gothic style and once the home of Sir Henry Chauncy, a Hertfordshire historian.

You continue past two other interesting houses; Walkern Bury Farm, sited near a Norman bailey with a deep ditch and bank **C**, and Walkern Hall **D**, a fine Regency mansion. From here, a tree-lined driveway leads into Benington.

IDYLLIC VILLAGE

The jettied, timber-framed cottages looking out over the duckpond and village green are the very essence of

►The village of Benington centres delightfully around its duckpond (above right) and the village green. St Peter's Church in the village contains tombs (left) of the de Benstede family.

14th-century porch, decorated with a crumbling St Michael slaying a dragon. The Benstede tombs and memorials are in the chancel, under the beautiful stonework of the arches built by Petronilla, widow of Sir John de Benstede, in 1330.

Later owners of the manor, the Caesars, are also commemorated here. Their name derives from an Italian doctor to Queen Mary and Queen Elizabeth; his successors,

along a hedgerow and fence, past a pond to another stile. Cross and continue ahead through a wide farm gateway. Go over a cross track and between two barns. Follow the track through the farmyard, crossing a ditch and bearing left by the last

building to a metal gate and waymarked stile. Cross and go ahead with a wood on your left, crossing another stile. At the corner of the wood, where a sweep of conifers goes off to the right, cross a stile and carry on through the trees into a field. Follow the woods on

the left to a road. Cross this and go straight on down a signposted path.

10► Bear right over a footbridge, then left to a wooden signpost. Turn right along a field edge. At the corner, go right, then soon left over a stile in the hedgerow. Continue on

through the meadows, keeping the river on your right, crossing stiles and tracks towards a mill ahead, until you emerge onto a road.

11► Turn left into Walkern, and go straight through the village to return to your starting point.

◄The Norman keep at Benington Lordship has carved stonework flanked by twin towers of flint.

fields and lanes returns you to Walkern, an interesting village of mixed houses and cottages of different ages. Worthy of particular note are the late 18th-century Mill House, built of bricks in two colours; the converted maltings and brewery house; the 17th-century chequered brick Manor House, with its lovely octagonal dovecote; the Elizabethan Rook's Nest Farm, with its fancy chimneys and mullioned windows; and the Old Rectory, built in 1632 for John Gorsuch, the rector of the time. Fairs were formerly a vital feature of village life, and were held opposite the 17th-century White Lion pub.

THE WITCH OF WENHAM

The most infamous inhabitant of Walkern was perhaps Jane Wenham, the Witch of Walkern, who lived in Church Lane. She was said to have bewitched sheep, servants and farm labourers, and was ducked in the pond before being committed to

▶*The old flour mills at Walkern, which have been pleasantly converted, were built in 1884 by C D Pearman.*

stand trial at Hertford Assizes in 1711. Evidence against her was given by three local clergymen as well as the historian Sir Henry Chauncy from Ardeley Bury.

The jury found her guilty and she was condemned to death. Although subsequently pardoned by Queen Anne, she was too frightened to return home, and lived for the rest of her life in Hertingfordbury under the protection of Earl Cowper. She was the last person in England to be sentenced to death for witchcraft, and her case was instrumental in bringing in the Witchcraft Act of 1735, which ruled that the 'crime' was no longer a capital offence.

following an elevation in their fortunes, owned the manor from 1614 up until 1741.

Next to the church are the flower-studded banks around the Norman keep of Benington Lordship **❻**, which looks down on the River Beane. A visit to the house and gardens here is probably the highlight of the walk (see box).

From the Lordship, a walk over

Built on a site occupied since Saxon times, the present manor house exhibits Georgian, Victorian and Edwardian influences.

Benington Lordship

Benington Lordship is set in a romantic garden established around the ruins of a Norman castle, a moat and a Victorian folly. A wonderful mixture of herbaceous planting, roses, trees and shrubs surrounds the house and cascades down a slope to ancient fish ponds.

There was an important church and royal palace here in Saxon times, thought to have been on the site of the present car park. William the Conqueror granted the manor to Peter de Valognes, whose son Roger enlarged the castle and built a stone keep in 1138. This was partly demolished by Henry II in 1177. Today, an outer bailey runs round the car park, the moat, the inner bailey and the flint ruins of the keep, which

is a listed monument, the only one of its kind in the county.

The present house was built around 1700 on the site of an Elizabethan farmhouse by the Caesar family, who owned the manor but lived at Benington Park, just outside the village. Sir John Chesshyre bought the estate in 1741 on the death of the last Caesar, and moved to the house when Benington Park burnt down.

The house was embellished in neo-Norman style in Victorian times, when the gatehouse, summer house and curtain wall were added. In the summer house is a tombstone of a Greek slave, and there is a Buddha in the niche above.

The estate was bought by the present owner's grandfather in 1905. He made further additions to the house, including the veranda, and planned the garden, whose Edwardian character is carefully retained.

SEVEN SPRINGS

A country walk round a village full of architectural interest

Ashwell has a long history. It lies on an old trade route, Ashwell Street, and is close by the important ancient highway, the Icknield Way. There is evidence of both Roman and Celtic settlements.

The *Domesday Book* points to it as one of the six most important towns in Hertfordshire, and in the Middle Ages it was a wealthy market town. For various reasons, it did not attain the stature of St Albans or Hertford, and today is no more than a substantial village. Its past, though, has bequeathed it many fine buildings. Pevsner, the architectural historian, wrote, 'the village has more architecturally worthwhile houses than any other in the county'.

The walk heads out of the village, via Ashwell Street and a quiet lane, to the gentle hills to the south. Here, there are wide views with long horizons and immense skies. Great sweeping fields cover the slopes.

The route heads back north past Arbury Banks **A**. From the ground, only the banks themselves can be seen, but aerial photographs have shown up stock enclosures and a possible Romano-Celtic temple, as well as defensive structures.

▲ *On the north side of Ashwell is Ashwell Bury, a fine house in grounds landscaped by Gertrude Jekyll.*

FACT FILE

✳	Ashwell, 5 miles (8km) north-east of Letchworth, off the A505
◻	Pathfinders 1049 (TL 23/33) and 1026 (TL 24/34), grid reference TL 271399

miles 0 1 2 3 4 5 6 7 8 9 10 miles
kms 0 1 2 3 4 5 6 7 8 9 10 11 12 13 14 15 kms

◔	Allow 2½ hours
▬	Tarmac roads and bridleways that can be muddy in parts. Gentle ascents and descents
P	Recreation ground opposite the cemetery at the eastern end of the village
T	An infrequent bus service links the village to Ashwell and Mordern BR station 2 miles (3.2km) away, Tel. (01462) 742292 for details
⧉	Three pubs and a tea-room in Ashwell
WC	By pavilion on recreation ground at the start
⌐	Ashwell Museum is open on Sundays and Bank Holidays, 2.30-5pm

North of the town, the fields are much neater and more compact. There are several fine houses, such as moated Ashwell End. Ashwell Bury, painted white with green shutters, was renovated by Sir Edwin Lutyens and has a garden designed by Gertrude Jekyll. Next to it are two renovated brewery buildings.

Back in the village, St Mary's Church **B** boasts a remarkable tower, at 176 feet (53.6m) the tallest in the county. This soaring edifice is topped with an octagonal lantern and a leaded spirelet, or spike, that is typical of Hertfordshire.

MEDIEVAL GRAFFITI

The church itself is also large, a testament to the medieval prosperity of Ashwell. The building is faced with Totternhoe stone, a soft clunch that weathers badly. Inside, the church is light and spacious. Etched in the walls of the tower are two pieces of 14th-century graffiti: an inscription in old Latin describing the aftermath of a plague in 1350, and another noting a dreadful tempest in 1361.

Nearby is an early Tudor town house, once used for collecting tithes for the Abbot of Westminster, and later as a meeting hall. It now contains Ashwell Museum **C**, which began life as a collection of curios

▼ *The ash tree gave its name to the village and still grows in the area.*

HERTFORDSHIRE

DEREK PRATT

DAVID WOODFALL/NHPA

THE WALK

ASHWELL

The walk begins from the recreation ground at the north-eastern end of the village.

1 Turn right and follow Station Road past the war memorial to Ashwell Street, a rutted track marked with a byway signpost.

2 Turn right and continue to a crossroads. Turn left uphill on a minor road between high banks. The lane flattens out on the brow of the hill. Keep on gently downhill. About 100 yards (90m) before a wood on your left, take a signposted track right, between fields, to a road. Turn left and continue for 350 yards (315m).

3 Take a signposted byway to your right by an old barn. Bear right by a long hedgerow, and continue on, uphill then down, for ¾ mile (1.2km), keeping the hedge on your right. As you near the

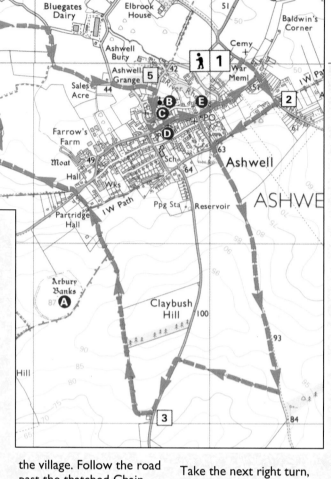

village, look left towards the fenced and partially hedged circle of Arbury Banks **A**. Continue, past the red-brick Partridge Hall on your left and Ashwell Street on your right, to a road. Turn right, then left, along Hinxworth Road by a house called West Point. After nearly 600 yards (540m), turn right on a signposted byway just before a bungalow. Follow this green lane until it meets a narrow road on a bend.

4 Go ahead a few paces on the road, then turn right over a stile by a footpath signpost. Follow the path towards some barn roofs. Cross a stile and turn right along a lane, which bears left towards

the village. Follow the road past the thatched Chain Cottage and look to the left at white-painted Ashwell Bury.

5 At a T-junction, turn right up Mill Street, to pass the church **B** and the Bushel and Strike pub.

Take the next right turn, by Ashwell Museum **C**, then take the next left to meet the High Street **D**. Turn left. Continue ahead, past the Springs Basin **E** on your left, and retrace your steps to the recreation ground at the start.

---

gathered by two village boys. When they grew up, they were instrumental in having the derelict building restored to house their ever-growing collection. The range of exhibits is amazing (extending even to a mummified black plague rat) and provides a unique record of village life from its earliest times.

▶ *Part of the 14th-century graffiti in the tower of St Mary's Church. As you return to the village, there is a good view (below left) of the church's elegant spirelet.*

The walk continues along the High Street **D**, which contains a number of Ashwell's best buildings. Among these are the 15th-century Kirby Manor, the Rose and Crown next door, and Bear House, whose rich internal timbering indicates the wealth of its builder.

Especially interesting are the 1476 Guildhall of St John the Baptist, now a baker's shop, and the pargetted Guildhouse of 1681 next door. Further on are Plait Hall, a timber-framed building once associated with the plaiting of straw for hats;

15th-century Forester's Cottages; and Jessamine House, formerly a farm and now the headquarters of the Veteran Car Club.

The final part of the walk passes the seven springs, which bubble out of the chalk into a pleasant pool — the Springs Basin **E** — before flowing off north to form the River Rhee, a tributary of the Cam. They are a Site of Special Scientific Interest, because the water contains a rare species of flatworm, and are surrounded by descendants of the ash trees that gave the town its name.

INDEX